Managing academic support services in universities

The convergence experience

Edited by
Terry Hanson

facet publishing

Published by
Facet Publishing
7 Ridgmount Street
London WC1E 7AE

Facet Publishing (formerly Library Association Publishing) is wholly owned by
CILIP: the Chartered Institute of Library and Information Professionals.

First published 2005

British Library Cataloguing in Publication Data
A catalogue record for this book is available from the British Library.

ISBN 1-85604-525-0

Typeset from editors' disks by Facet Publishing in 11/13 Elegant Garamond
and Humanist 521.
Printed and made in Great Britain by MPG Books Ltd, Bodmin, Cornwall.

Contents

Contributors

Professor Mark Clark, Director of Information Systems, University of Manchester.

Sue Clegg, Director of Information Services, Roehampton University.

Mel Collier, Acting Chief Librarian, University of Leuven, Belgium, and Professor at the University of Northumbria.

Sheila Corrall, Professor of Librarianship and Information Management, University of Sheffield, and formerly Director of Academic Services at the University of Southampton.

Tom Crawshaw, Director of Information Services, University of Surrey.

Vic Elliott, Director, Scholarly Information Services and University Librarian, Australian National University.

Clive D. Field, Director of Scholarship and Collections at the British Library.

Cathryn Gallacher, Assistant Director of Information Services, University of Bristol.

Margaret Haines, Director of Information Services and Systems, King's College London.

Terry Hanson, Director of Information Services, University College Chichester.

Larry Hardesty, Dean of the Library, University of Nebraska at Kearney, USA.

Helen Hayes, Vice-Principal for Knowledge Management and Librarian, University of Edinburgh.

Mike Hopkins, Director of Information Services, University of Wales Aberystwyth.

Professor Derek Law, Librarian and Head of the Information Resources Directorate, University of Strathclyde.

Nigel Macartney, Director of Information Services, the University of Ulster.

Di Martin, Dean of Learning and Information Services, University of Hertfordshire.

Patricia Methven, Director of Archives and Information Management, King's College London.

Janet Peters, Director of Library and Information Services, University of Wales Newport.

Michele Shoebridge, Director of Information Services, University of Birmingham.

Nick Smith, Director of Library and Information Services, Aston University.

Ali Taylor, Assistant Vice Chancellor, University of the West of England, Bristol.

Mark Toole, Director of Information Services, University of Brighton.

Christopher West, Director of Library and Information Services, University of Wales Swansea.

Jean Yeoh, Head of ISS Corporate Services, King's College London.

1

Introduction: twenty years of convergence in the UK

Terry Hanson

What is convergence?

In Chapter 2 Clive Field describes convergence in the following way: 'Convergence is used to describe the situation in which the library and academic computing services, with or without other services, are brought together for managerial purposes under a common full-time executive director generally recruited from a professional information background.'

As such, convergence has been with us for almost 20 years, and it seems a good time to reflect on the nature of this experience; to ask whether it is a successful model, and one that is here to stay; or whether, in another 20 years, it will be seen as a passing phase, as a medium-term response to a set of circumstances prevailing during the early years of the computing revolution.

Either way, a significant proportion of UK higher education institutions is currently converged (using a broad definition, of which more later) and, according to our representative sample of case studies, fairly content with their lot and keen to perpetuate the model.

A successful model?

How can we know whether the model has been, or is currently, successful? And further, can we take a collective – national – approach to this question or should we confine the assessment to individual universities and their local circumstances?

Well, the short answer to the first question is that there are no clear, unambiguous, universally acceptable criteria by which we can say that convergence either does or does not deliver the goods. It all depends on your perspective, and there are several to consider: those of the vice-chancellor and other senior university managers, those of the customers of the converged service, whether students or staff, and those of the staff involved in the converged operation themselves.

Clearly, on a simple level we can observe, quite unambiguously, that the main determinant of whether convergence is introduced or abandoned, and whether it is successful or not, is the vice-chancellor and his or her judgement in the current local circumstances. The vice-chancellor will reach judgement from the perspective of the entire university. It is not just a question for the two professions most involved, because convergence deals with the strategic issue of university-wide information management.

So, following this logic, the fact that there is so much convergence in the UK is due to the foresight and wisdom of vice-chancellors and principals. They will have been influenced by many factors, not least of which was the Follett report (Joint Funding Councils' Libraries Review Group, 1993), which pointed out some of the advantages of the converged approach, particularly from a strategic planning point of view. Perhaps even more influential, however, was their own perception of the growing strategic importance of IT and the need to ensure that it is aligned with corporate strategy. Many vice-chancellors and principals chose to resolve this issue by what we now call convergence, but at the time it was in many cases a pragmatic move aimed at bringing greater strategic oversight to the management of library and, in particular, computing services.

It so happened that a number of university librarians and IT directors, though mainly the former (Law, 1998), were on hand who were thinking along similar lines and eager to grasp the opportunity of playing a broader role. Librarians could certainly see that they were increasingly dependent on the IT department even if the reverse were not necessarily true. But they could also see the broader potential for taking a strategic approach to information management.

From the perspective of the vice-chancellor we may reasonably conclude that the converged model has delivered the goods, or at least some of them, if only because the model has persisted. It has done so in most institutions (Aston (Discombe, 2003), Northumbria and Southampton notwithstanding) at that crucial time when the incumbent director of information services has vacated the post, and thus provided an opportunity for a rethink. We will consider this matter from the perspective of the heads of the converged services a little later.

Given the centrality of the vice-chancellor in the transition to and from convergence it would have been useful and very interesting to have included their perspective directly through a survey or a couple of case studies. This was considered and rejected. It was rejected because the perspective can be readily discerned through the accounts of how convergence came into being that are included in this book. And also because the perspective was, inevitably and correctly, a very broad one.

It was my purpose in designing this book to address the convergence experience in greater detail and the best way to achieve this was to concentrate on the perspective of those who were charged with implementing and managing converged services. And even though the carefully considered arguments of a highly able and experienced director of information services may be blown away in an instant by a new vice-chancellor, it is nonetheless the detailed observations of these convergence leaders that, I feel, gives us the most useful perspective on the convergence experience. For it is the *experience* of convergence that we are most concerned with, not just the initial decision-making process with all of its attendant political and pragmatic considerations.

This being so, some 16 case studies were commissioned for this book: 12 from converged institutions, two from de-converged institutions and two from universities that rejected convergence following a thorough examination of it as a possible model for adoption. Among the group of 12 convergence case studies there is a mix of large and small institutions and of new and old universities. There are also three overview chapters discussing the extent and nature of convergence in other parts of the world: Australia, the USA and Europe outside the UK.

Each of the case study authors was asked to adopt a common approach, or structure, for their papers. This was not rigidly applied but it was seen as important in order that there would a basis for comparison as well as a reasonable basis to inform questions about whether convergence was and is more or less suited to the different types (size, age, complexity) of institution.

What then can we learn from this collective experience?

How and why convergence came about

The general picture that emerges is of a recognition by senior management of the need to exercise greater strategic control and direction over the converging areas of IT and library services. More particularly there was a concern to ensure that:

- the emerging, and exciting, developments in areas such as e-learning, institutional information systems (portals) and access to online information resources should be harnessed effectively; this would require contributions from staff in several different areas.
- future provision of information services needed to be more customer – student – focused, with an emphasis on convenience; for many, this meant one-stop-shops and integrated service points.

Many of these senior managers were clearly influenced by the Follett (Joint Funding Councils) and Fielden (John Fielden Consultancy) reports of 1993. And, having decided to at least look at the possibility of convergence, several institutions conducted careful investigations of experience elsewhere and/or called in external consultants to assist them in their decision-making processes. It was also common practice to establish a working party to conduct the invest-igations and make the high-level recommendation and/or to take forward the detailed work of implementation once the decision to converge had been taken.

However, no matter how clear the conviction in favour of convergence, the principal influence, in practical terms, was frequently that of actual or impending vacancies in the key positions of head of library services and head of computing services. This was often the catalyst for, or simply the opportunity to engage in, serious discussion. Other local circumstances seen as catalysts have been physical changes, mergers with other institutions and, very importantly, the promise of a new building.

Apart from the general reasons adduced in favour of convergence noted above, the principal advantages associated with convergence, according to our case studies, are:

- a clear strategic direction governing all of the converged services
- a combined budget covering all of these areas
- a place on the university's senior management group, ideally, for the director
- an opportunity to forge a common customer-focused service ethos
- an opportunity to plan and design new service delivery models based on user convenience, one-stop-shops, integrated learning centres, integrated service points, and so on.

What is included?

As expected there was a great deal of variation in terms of the other departments and sections, beyond the library and computing services, that were included in the converged department. Services such as learning technology, media services, support for classrooms were frequently included. Other services included reprographics and printing services, telephone services, university presses and careers services.

In many ways the most interesting question in this area of discussion relates to the administrative computing (or MIS) function. In many universities there has been a stronger relationship between this service area and the main administrative departments such as finance and registry than with the rest of IT services. And in some cases, in spite of the general logic of convergence, administrative computing has, at least initially, been left out of the mix.

However, it is also interesting to note that eventually this service does become part of the converged department. Certainly, given the strategic importance of systems integration to major project areas such as e-learning and portal development, the administrative computing team is a crucial component.

Models of convergence

The case study authors were asked to describe their model of convergence by reference to a simple classification:

- *Model 1: oversight at pro-vice-chancellor level*. Common reporting line for the heads of library services and of computing services, and perhaps others; otherwise separate services, with or without good co-operation between the heads.
- *Model 2: strategic co-ordination*. A senior post of director (or dean or pro-vice-chancellor) of information services exercises active co-ordination; considerable autonomy is given to each area within an agreed strategic framework with significant levels of interdependence and co-operation; there is perhaps limited integration at the service level.
- *Model 3: service-level convergence*. Like Model 2 but with significant levels of service integration perhaps to the point where roles and titles have been re-defined.

While noting that there is a constant change and adaptation process in place at all 12 universities it is clear that half of them have adopted something close to Model 2 while the other half have either adopted and implemented Model 3 or are moving fairly rapidly towards doing so. This is interesting as an indicator of the relative strength of the customer service argument in favour of convergence. For, whereas the main influence behind Model 2 appears to be the need for strategic co-ordination, the additional motivation to move towards Model 3 is the need to focus on the front-line needs of students and other customers.

Experience

Perhaps it comes as no surprise to discover that 12 directors of information services, when asked, said they liked the converged model and they thought it was successful and here to stay. This certainly tells us something about their personal preferences but they typically acknowledge the difficulties in reaching clear conclusions when evaluating their experience.

And principal among these difficulties is the fact that it cannot be known what might have been achieved without convergence. It is also difficult, as discussed briefly above, to establish clear criteria and a methodology for determining how successful the experiment has been. Surveys of users will be helpful only if the users concerned have experience of what had gone before. But even then, they too will be unable to know how things might have been without convergence.

Notwithstanding these difficulties, our converged service directors are consistent in their general evaluations. They note the following particular benefits of convergence, in practice as well as in theory:

- the opportunity to take an integrated, or holistic, approach to the strategic planning and management of academic support services
- the converged structure facilitates, rather than inhibits, the development of cross-sectional initiatives such as the implementation of e-learning or of an institutional portal
- the opportunity to establish standardized approaches to service delivery and customer service in general
- opportunities for economies of scale and resource sharing.

The nature and role of the director of information services

The vision of convergence, as espoused by its advocates (for instance Law, 1998), was, and is, predicated on the existence of a group of individuals who, if they existed at all, did so in spite of the professional development routes then available. Indeed, there is still no formal education, training and development infrastructure for a director of information services. Nor is there a professional body to bring them together and represent them. (It is interesting to note here that in Ireland there is no convergence at the institutional level whereas there is a very successful annual conference of the Irish Universities Information Services Colloquium to encourage a joint approach and mutual understanding among library, IT and other related professionals. In Britain, by contrast, there is a great deal of convergence at the institutional level but very little in terms of national professional activity.)

These early directors of converged services found themselves in these positions because they had the strategic awareness of the potential contribution of the combined operation and the management skills to bring two, or more, departments, often with very different cultures, together. The former required an understanding and appreciation of the reach and potential of IT in higher education. As Les Watson, writing in *Ariadne* in 1998, noted:

staff who position themselves at the junctions of information management, C&IT, and most crucially learning development will be best placed to make the most significant future contribution. They will need an understanding of information based activities, including C&IT, combined with a knowledge of, and active involvement in, student learning.

But it is perhaps the management challenges that are the most significant, at least initially, when moving to a converged model. As the case studies in this book illustrate there is enormous potential for friction and distrust as different professions with their different cultures come together. The successful director of information services is likely to be one who:

- has a strong commitment to the convergence model
- develops a clear strategy with clear goals
- exercises leadership
- has strong support from senior university management
- is customer focused
- is a good communicator and a good listener
- is patient
- has a genuine appreciation of the potential contribution of all members and groups within the converged department
- is able to build and motivate cross-sectional teams
- is, to paraphrase Norman Higham (former Librarian of Bristol University), a university man (or woman) first and a librarian or IT professional second.

Is convergence here to stay?

As noted above, the answer to this question lies with university vice-chancellors. However, as suggested in our case studies, there is, in addition to enthusiasm for the converged model, a healthy degree of circumspection regarding this question. And this is not just because the authors know it will not be their decision.

Many make the point that there is no simple standard model that can be applied to universities of a particular size or type. Note, for example, that Birmingham and Bristol universities have adopted convergence but another large civic university, Manchester, chose not to, having undertaken a thorough review of the options. Indeed Mark Clark in his case study includes among his concluding remarks the observation that 'World-class institutions do not have converged services' (see Chapter 17, p.157).

There is also a recognition that, even if they suggest that the converged service is greater than the sum of its parts, the individual sections are more than capable of doing the right things and achieving a great deal. There is no limit to what can be achieved when people work together in a spirit of mutual respect and determination. This is, after all, the principal argument in favour of convergence but it doesn't mean that formal convergence is the only way.

We may, as suggested in the opening paragraph of this chapter, look back in future on convergence as a solution to a problem at a particular time. But, I would suggest that, by whatever name and in whatever configuration, the essentials of convergence (integrated planning at the strategic level and some level of customer-driven integration at the service level and a great deal of inter-professional co-operation in between) will remain.

And finally . . .

As noted in many of the case studies the HEFCE requirement that all universities produce and maintain an information strategy (Brindley, 1998) was an important factor in the development of convergence. There was much uncertainty at the time regarding this requirement but the general thrust of the initiative was that, as universities are highly dependent on information then it would follow that an improvement in the way that information was managed would benefit the organization generally.

Thus it was recommended that, as a first step, universities needed to analyse their information flows and processes and to develop a more sophisticated model of their requirements. Such a model would emphasize important principles such as:

- ensuring that information resources are created once and shared as necessary rather than duplicated
- bureaucratic processes that are founded upon outdated models of information processing should be redesigned.

Essentially the information strategy initiative encouraged a horizontal (information management) perspective on the organization. As such, this was a very useful analytical tool and one that encouraged a greater appreciation of the strategic importance of information as a resource. And, whereas it is important that this consideration should continue to be at the forefront of management and strategic planning – not just a one-off analytical tool – the institutional committee devoted to information management may not be the best forum to ensure that requirement.

The machinery of strategic planning and decision-making works through vertical processes: through line management, through senior management groups and through process committees for key areas such as learning and teaching or research. Thus, if the information services department wishes to promote, say, e-learning, the most effective approach would be to ensure that the initiative is owned and championed by those (people and committees) charged with the responsibility for learning and teaching. If it is seen that the information services department and the information management committee are driving the initiative there is a danger that it will be seen as IT-led, and inappropriately so. The 'e' should be removed from e-learning: it is a learning issue.

Of course, there will be information services committees that avoid this pitfall successfully, perhaps by a combination of senior management involvement, a very clear brief that does not overlap too much with other process-based committees and, perhaps most importantly, a significant degree of clout in terms of resource allocation. For those that do not, it is imperative that the information services staff ensure that they are integrated into the vertical, process-based policy and decision-making machinery. In this way they can help ensure that policies and initiatives are IT-influenced, as they need to be, without being IT-led.

References

Brindley, L. (1998) Information Strategies. In Hanson, T. and Day, J. (eds) *Managing the Electronic Library*, London, Bowker Saur, 27–48.

Discombe, R. (2003) *Convergence of Information Resource Services in UK Universities*, unpublished MA dissertation, Brighton, Brighton University.

John Fielden Consultancy (1993) *Supporting Expansion: a report on human resource management in academic libraries, for the Joint Funding Councils' Libraries Review Group*, Bristol: HEFCE.

Joint Funding Councils' Libraries Review Group (1993) *Report* (the Follett Report), Bristol, HEFCE.

Kelly, P. (1988) Information Management: an academic context, *British Journal of Academic Librarianship*, 3 (3), 122–35.

Law, D. (1998) Convergence of Academic Support Services. In Hanson, T. and Day, J. (eds), *Managing the Electronic Library*, London, Bowker Saur, 49–62.

Watson, L. (1998) Information Services: a mission and a vision, *Ariadne*, 14. Reprinted in Pugh, L, MacColl, J. and Dempsey, L. (eds) *Delivering the Electronic Library: an Ariadne reader*, The Ariadne Project, 1999, 31–3.

2

A history of convergence in United Kingdom universities

Clive D. Field

This paper reviews the extent and nature of convergence of information services in the United Kingdom higher education sector. It traces the history of the process since the 1980s and considers the principal drivers behind it.

The extent of convergence

As the theory and practice described in the literature make clear, convergence is a term to which multiple meanings can be attached. It is as well, therefore, to commence our own review with an agreed definition. Some writers (John Fielden Consultancy, 1993, 15; Sykes and Gerrard, 1997, 68) have distinguished between 'organisational or formal convergence', in which services are brought together for management purposes; and 'operational or informal convergence', in which the detailed functions or operations of the services are changed or merged. They have pointed out that it is not strictly necessary to have organizational convergence for operational convergence to take place; for instance, heads of services can work collaboratively – say, on joint strategic planning, end-user training, or provision of student computers – without any integration of management occurring. It is also the case that services can be organizationally converged while making slow progress with converging operationally.

Combining organizational and operational convergence, it would be hard to find many United Kingdom higher education institutions without some manifestation of converged behaviour. Accordingly, a rather strict definition has been applied here, whereby convergence is used to describe the situation in which the library and academic computing services, with or without other services, are brought together for managerial purposes under a common full-time executive director generally recruited from a professional information background. This maps on to the executive director model of convergence identified by Royan (1994, 18), while ignoring his four alternative models (goodwill and commonsense; peer co-ordinator; common chairperson; and common reporting to a pro-vice-chancellor or deputy principal), and on to the definition recently propounded by Pugh (1997b, 50).

This restricted definition of convergence, centred on the merger of library and academic computing services under a single executive director, is important, since it dates the origins of convergence to the mid-1980s. The integrated academic services pioneered by Brighton and Plymouth polytechnics in the mid-1970s were not converged on this criterion, since the learning resource centres, through which they were integrated, combined library, media and educational development within a common organization but excluded computing (doubtless sensibly so at that stage, when the brief of computing was very limited, confined to number-crunching for scientists and to a few key administrative systems). Thinking and practice on 'true' convergence, based upon the concept of the 'chief information officer', can be traced back to around 1980 in the USA, with early implementations at Columbia University, Carnegie Mellon University, California State University at Chico and the Virginia Polytechnic Institute. Paradoxically, although convergence began in the USA, it has been proportionately more pervasive in the UK. One of the first British pioneers of convergence was St Andrew's College of Education in Glasgow, where the process was described by Gray (1986). Other early implementers between 1987 and 1989 whose experiences have been described in the literature were Plymouth (Sidgreaves, 1988), Salford (Harris, 1988) and Stirling (Annan, 1992; Davis, 1998; Royan, 1990) universities. It was symptomatic of the professional interest generated by convergence in the UK that the *British Journal of Academic Librarianship* devoted a theme issue to it as soon as 1988.

To start with, convergence was principally identified with what is now described as the 'new' university sector – the pre-1992 polytechnics covered in Sutherland's survey for the Council of Polytechnic Librarians in 1992, or the smaller and more recently established of the 'old' (pre-1992) universities. However, as can be seen by the celebrated defensive letter from Fred Ratcliffe and David Hartley, respectively Librarian and Director of the University Computing Service at Cambridge, to the *Times Higher Education Supplement* in March 1993 (Ratcliffe and Hartley, 1993), even the ancient universities were becoming aware of the trend to converge. While recognizing the growing complementarity of the library and computing services, Ratcliffe and Hartley cautioned against their 'wedlock' and ended up with the extraordinary *ex cathedra* statement that: 'At the very least the priorities and management needs in two such diverse bodies are incompatible.' Within a matter of months, the ground had been somewhat removed from under their feet by the steer towards convergence given by the Follett enquiry into higher education libraries. The main Follett report (Joint Funding Councils' Libraries Review Group, 1993, 28–9) noted that 'there are many advantages in organizational convergence', even though it acknowledged that each institution had to determine its own approach. The subsidiary report on human resource management issues (John Fielden Consultancy, 1993, 22–3) predicted increasing organizational convergence and near universal operational convergence, at one level or another. The very substantial library and learning resource centre building programme that followed on from Follett, as one of the principal outcomes of his report, certainly greatly facilitated operational convergence, in enabling increased co-location of library, media and computer user services. At least one computing service director (Haworth, 1994, 98–9) felt called to question what she regarded as Follett's somewhat uncritical endorsement of convergence and asked to see the reasoned case for his Committee's recommendation.

Various studies during the past decade have documented the spread of convergence in the UK higher education sector. Royan (1994, 18) found 35 institutions operating on an information supremo model, with a further eight actively considering moving in the same direction; 24 of them gathered for the first residential meeting of heads of merged services, held at Buxton in September 1994, which Royan was instrumental in organizing. Three years later, figures from Pugh's questionnaire survey of the entire sector in January 1997 would suggest that around 50 universities and colleges had converged; based on a 70% response from the 162 institutions approached, Pugh reported that 42.5% had converged according to his (and my) definition, with another 11.9% actively planning it. Of these, two-fifths had converged during 1988–93 and three-fifths since 1994 or were planning convergence, with 31% declaring the achievement of full convergence (embracing technological, managerial, administrative, operational and physical integration), 18% describing more federal arrangements for service co-ordination, and 50% still being at an evolutionary stage, sometimes missing a critical element such as physical convergence (Pugh, 1997a, 26, 29, 41; 1997b, 65).

By May 2001, to judge from directory information published on the web by the Standing Conference of National and University Libraries (SCONUL) and the Universities and Colleges Information Systems Association (UCISA) and collated by the author, the number of converged and non-converged institutions was roughly equal, at 66 and 68 respectively. The most converged part of the sector were the higher education colleges (61%), followed by pre-1992 universities other than those in the Consortium of Research Libraries in the British Isles (CURL) (55%), CURL institutions (45% with an executive information director) and 'new' universities (38%). The lower percentage among the former polytechnics may partly reflect the limitations of the web-based survey (some of the directory entries are ambiguous), and/or the relative narrowness of our definition, but is nevertheless interesting, given their close historic identity with the convergence process; Pugh (1997a, 27–8) then had them out-converging the old universities, by 54% to 40%.

Occasional examples of de-convergence, separating libraries and computing services, can be found at Luton in 1997 (Stone, 1998), at Northumbria in 2000, at Aston (Discombe, 2003) in 2002 and Southampton in 2003.

The nature of convergence

Within this overall picture of the growth of convergence, considerable diversity may be observed in the title of the merged service and its head, the degree of inclusivity in the service make-up, and the internal structures of the service. Royan (1994, 19), for example, discovered no fewer than 17 different service names in the converged environment, and, while information services was the most common, it had still been adopted by only a minority of converging institutions. Much the same is probably true now. 'Director' is the post title most often reserved for the head of service, but even here there are many exceptions; at Birmingham, 'librarian and director of information services' is employed, since it was felt important, for reasons of university statutes and politics, not to lose the 'librarian' element. Within the UK at least, it is notable that the majority of heads of converged services have been recruited from professional library backgrounds. Royan (1994, 20) reported that 18 of 27 heads of merged library and computing services were librarians, and Pugh (1997a, 38; 1997b, 64) that 63% of converged services were led by librarians, 10% by computer managers, and 8% by academics. Law (1998, 54) found that 'nationally the ratio of appointments appears to run at perhaps 5:1 in favour of librarians'.

The inclusion list for merged services is equally susceptible to great variety, with a SCONUL investigation (Bainton, 1997) permitting no fewer than 15 different service permutations, including a miscellaneous category. The presence of libraries and academic computing services in converged organizations is, of course, required by our working definition. Beyond this, if the May 2001 survey is correct, about two-thirds also have responsibility for administrative computing or management information services (historically often the preserve of the registrar or equivalent) and three-fifths for media and related (increasingly technology-assisted learning) services. Telephony is also frequently converged. Especially in smaller and newer institutions, where lack of critical mass may inhibit the degree of professional differentiation that is possible, many student support services may be bundled into the convergence:

careers, catering, chaplaincy, counselling, healthcare, housing and nursery services can all be found co-managed with library, computing and other learning services. About a fifth of converged services seem to have this sort of role. Yet, even in large and more traditional universities, the inclusion list for a converged service can be long and broad.

Given such diversity, it is not surprising that converged services are organized on many different management lines, making it difficult to discern overall patterns, still less to identify a possible blueprint for others to follow. Perhaps this is not altogether undesirable, since, in the final analysis, the structural implementation of convergence will owe much to the local political, cultural, financial and spatial circumstances in any given institution. However, one broad distinction may be observed. That is whether the internal arrangements of a converged service under a single executive director follow closely the contours of previous format-based (for instance, library, academic computing) approaches or whether a genuinely integrated structure is adopted, mixing and matching within new management units skills and expertise from a range of information professions. In 1994 Royan (1994, 19) found that only a third of his information supremos were managing their services in a truly integrated fashion. Three years later, Pugh (1997a, 42–3) detected more progress in adopting boundary-spanning structures that broke down distinctions between services (63% as against 37% of services that adhered to more conventional service boundaries). In May 2001 32 of 66 converged services seemed to have a fairly traditional service structure, at least superficially (with preservation of an identifiably separate librarian being one obvious criterion), while 34 had a more boundary-spanning structure. Although nine of the 20 British universities in CURL had converged by this date, all but two were on very cautious lines, to the extent that they still had an identifiable librarian.

Drivers for convergence

The circumstances that result in an institution's decision to converge (or not) are complex and variable and ultimately specific to the institution concerned, making generalization difficult. As an example, we may note Field's account (1996, 34) of the thinking of the University of Birmingham:

> The rationale for doing so was felt to lie in the need to maximize the potential of information technology, to facilitate the transition from teaching to learning, to foster the development of generic skills amongst students, to heighten the awareness and skills of academic staff about information issues, to reflect the increasing functional overlap between service providers, to counter a lack of strategic and

operational co-ordination between providers, to address certain deficiencies in management structures and service provision, and to optimize the use of resources at a time of decline in real levels of funding.

That said, it is possible to separate out the underlying factors which have been most commonly cited as determinants of convergence within UK higher education and to categorize them into three: those which are truly universal; those that are particularly relevant within the UK; and those that apply mainly at individual institutional level.

Not unnaturally, the principal global driver since the mid-1980s has been an increasing convergence of the technologies for producing, storing, retrieving, processing and transmitting text, data, image and voice, and the associated increasing dependence of libraries on electronic information and network infrastructure. Under these circumstances, it no longer makes sense for investment and management of the technical infrastructure to be fragmented between different service providers, nor for information (whether purchased or institutionally created) to be hoarded and not shared. The advent of the world wide web has produced a lowest common denominator for presenting information in a seamless fashion; the increasing popularity of managed learning environments such as WebCT or Blackboard has provided a framework in which a whole range of electronic information for students can be integrated and made interactive; and the development of hybrid libraries has shown how traditional information formats may co-exist with the electronic.

An especially important content convergence breakthrough in UK universities has been the recognition that administrative information systems (finance, student records, personnel and so forth) can no longer be seen as the exclusive preserve of the administration. Those systems, and the key data which underpin them, are increasingly required by staff, students and other service pro-viders. In this way, institutions are realizing the imperative for a single technical infrastructure to underpin all information needs, and for a holistic approach to the acquisition, creation, dissemination and preservation of content. Given such a scenario, what more natural outcome than to seek to place the management and delivery of both infrastructure and content into a single set of professional hands?

Within the UK these overarching technological and information drivers have been given added impetus by the policies of Government and the four higher education funding councils, which provide much of the finance for universities and colleges in England, Wales, Scotland and Northern Ireland. On the Government's part, regardless of political flavour, and reflected in funding council allocations, has been the commitment throughout the 1990s rapidly to expand student numbers (with a 50% participation rate by the eligible age group now on the horizon) in ways which address lifelong learning, widening access and social inclusion, the development of transferable skills and employability of students, and which shift the emphasis from didactic teaching to self-paced learning. All this has had to be delivered without any commensurate increase in real-term resources (indeed, unit costs per student have fallen dramatically on the whole). At the same time, the abolition of student maintenance grants, the introduction of student tuition fees and the general spread in society of a 'customer is king' philosophy have meant that the expectations which students and their parents have of the higher education system have increased. Integrated, effective and 'one-stop shop' provision of facilities in general, and of information and learning resources in particular, is increasingly essential, if institutions are to cope with the needs of a much larger, more diversified and more demanding student population. Much of this context is evident from the massive report of the National Committee of Inquiry into Higher Education, chaired by Lord Dearing, and published under the title *Higher Education in the Learning Society* (1997).

Funding councils have sought to underpin these policy objectives by a variety of mechanisms to cajole or encourage institutions to comply with them. A particular characteristic of the UK has been the need for conformity with a national framework for quality assurance and accountability, largely delivered through the Quality Assurance Agency. Through that Agency institutions have been subject both to periodic across-the-board inspections and to reviews of individual subject provision, both of which include a major emphasis on learning infrastructure and resourcing. For research, there is a similar audit process, in the form of the peer-review-based Research Assessment Exercise. The funding councils require institutions to prepare and publish, and to monitor the implementation of, strategic plans covering all of these areas. The compilation of a formal institutional learning and teaching strategy, for example, with clearly articulated deliverables, is now mandatory. Commencing with the Follett report in 1993, and facilitated by the Information Strategies Steering Group of the Joint Information Systems Committee established in 1994, universities and colleges have similarly been fairly heavily steered towards the production of integrated information strategies. This initiative, in bringing institutional management and service providers together with a common purpose, has been a driver for a good deal of organizational and operational convergence in the UK.

At the end of the day, convergence occurs in an individual university or college, and it is the cumulative impact of these external (international and national) drivers on institutional management which counts. To imply that the convergence decision is driven by institutional management is correct, for Pugh (1997a, 29–30, 36; 1997b, 56–9) has demonstrated that convergence in the UK is in reality very largely a top-down management process, usually initiated from the institutional centre and often implemented in only a partially consultative manner; in so far as service providers had any influence on decision-making, he found that libraries were more often involved than computer centres. It is hard to think of very many working examples of the collaborative and participative user-driven convergence which Collier (1996) favoured. Given this management-led approach, it is perhaps surprising, in view of the worsening economic position of higher education in the 1990s, that cost-cutting or the achievement of economies of scale through aggregation of service has not weighed more heavily in pushing forward convergence. This was again demonstrated by Pugh's research (1997a, 36–9); 48% of converged services reported that budgets had actually increased after convergence, while 55% saw growth in their staffing establishment. The Birmingham experience bore this out, particularly on the human resourcing side; the costs of establishing new hybrid posts, of giving personal protection of salaries to those displaced by convergence, and of funding early retirement and voluntary severance packages were high – and only met by judicious use of budget centre reserves and vacancy savings. At the same time, the consolidation of budgets from so many historically discrete service areas did provide much-needed opportunities for virement, rationalization and cross-subsidy.

As to timing, institutions have often chosen to act on convergence when a natural vacancy occurs; or when there is a performance issue or lack of confidence in one particular service or its head (a common perception has been the failing of some academic computing services to develop a service ethos at a rate sufficient to meet the increasingly mass higher education market for information technology applications and services). Hence the prediction of the John Fielden Consultancy (1993, 22–3): 'Organizational convergence will continue to take place, but it will be driven largely by personal and political factors within each institution.'

Acknowledgement

This chapter was published originally as the first half of a paper entitled: Theory and Practice: Reflections on Convergence in United Kingdom Universities (in *Liber Quarterly*, 11, 267–89, 2001). It has been slightly amended for inclusion in this collection. We are very grateful to the author and to K. G. Saur, the publishers of *Liber Quarterly*, for their permission to include the paper in this book.

References

Annan, A. (1992) The Management of Change in Information Services, *Campus Information: the Electronic Answer? Papers presented at the Second IUCC/SCONUL Conference held at the Heathlands Hotel, Bournemouth, 22–24 June 1992*, London, IUCC/SCONUL, 151–7.

Bainton, T. (1997) *Results of Convergence Survey*, 1997, London, Standing Conference of National and University Libraries.

Collier, M. (1996) The Context of Convergence. In Oldroyd, M. (ed.), *Staff Development in Academic Libraries: present practice and future challenges*, London, Library Association Publishing.

Davis, R. (1998) Case Study: University of Stirling. In Hanson, T. and Day, J. (eds), *Managing the Electronic Library: a practical guide for information professionals*, London, Bowker Saur, 109–25.

Discombe, R. (2003) *Convergence of Information Resource Services in UK Universities*, unpublished MA dissertation, Brighton, Brighton University.

Field, C. D. (1996) Implementing Convergence at the University of Birmingham, *SCONUL Newsletter*, **9**, 33–7.

Foster, A. (1995) The Emergence of Convergence, *Library Manager*, **11** (October), 12–13.

Gray, P. (1986) Integrating Computing into Learning Resources in a College of Education, *Learning Resources Journal*, **2** (3), 109–15.

Harris, C. (1988) Academic Information Services at the University of Salford, *British Journal of Academic Librarianship*, **3** (3), 147–52.

Haworth, A. (1994) The Follett Report: a computer services perspective, *British Journal of Academic Librarianship*, **9** (1/2), 97–104.

John Fielden Consultancy (1993) *Supporting Expansion: a report on human resource management in academic libraries, for the Joint Funding Councils' Libraries Review Group*, Bristol, HEFCE.

Joint Funding Councils' Libraries Review Group (1993) *Report* (the Follett Report), Bristol, HEFCE.

Kelly, P. (1988) Information Management: an academic context, *British Journal of Academic Librarianship*, **3** (3), 122–35.

Law, D. (1998) Convergence of Academic Support Services. In Hanson, T. and Day, J. (eds), *Managing the Electronic Library: a practical guide for information professionals*, London, Bowker Saur, 49–62.

National Committee of Inquiry into Higher Education (1997) *Higher Education in the Learning Society* (the Dearing Report), London, HMSO.

Pugh, L. C. (1997a) *Convergence in Academic Support Services*, British Library Research and Innovation Report, 54, London, British Library Research and Innovation Centre.

Pugh, L. C. (1997b) Some Theoretical Bases of Convergence, *New Review of Academic Librarianship*, **3**, 49–66.

Ratcliffe, F. W. and Hartley, D. (1993) Library Services, *Times Higher Education Supplement*, 5 March 1993, 17.

Royan, B. (1990) Staff Structures for Today's Information Services, *British Journal of Academic Librarianship*, **5** (3), 165–9.

Royan, B. (1994) Are You Being Merged? A survey of convergence in information service provision, *SCONUL Newsletter*, **1**, 17–20.

Sidgreaves, I. D. (1988) The Development of 'Academic Services' at Polytechnic South West, *British Journal of Academic Librarianship*, **3** (3), 136–46.

Stone, T. (1998) (De)converged Services at Luton, *SCONUL Newsletter*, **14**, 40–1.

Sykes, P. and Gerrard, S. (1997) Operational Convergence at Roehampton Institute London and Liverpool John Moores University, *New Review of Academic Librarianship*, **3**, 67–89.

3

Breaking the mould: convergence at the University of Wales Aberystwyth

Mike Hopkins

Origins

Convergence is one of those 'c' words, like co-operation, collaboration and compliance, which become shorthand for sometimes emotive themes that at different times dominate the headlines and set the professional agenda. Ten years ago the Follett report did just that with its recommendation that 'each institution should fundamentally reassess the way in which it plans and provides for the information needs of those working within it, and the place of the Library in meeting those needs' (Joint Funding Councils' Libraries Review Group, 1993). At the University of Wales Aberystwyth (UWA) this particular proposal provoked special interest since it was known that the University Librarian and the Head of the Computer Unit were both due to retire in the next few years, each after more than two decades in charge. It was consequently decided to establish the 'Working Party on post-Follett Information Strategy' (the Working Party), under the chairmanship of a pro-vice-chancellor, to consider future managerial arrangements for the delivery of high quality information services. Its subsequent report duly recommended that the University Library, the Computer Unit and the Audio-Visual Services Unit be merged to create a single organization under the direction of a Director of Information Services.

Although both Library and computing staff at UWA expressed varying degrees of caution, doubt and even suspicion about convergence, the Working Party was persuaded by the advantages highlighted in the Follett report and the associated Fielden report (John Fielden Consultancy, 1993) and endorsed the establishment of an integrated information service. The University was already giving tentative attention to the need for an inclusive information strategy and the establishment of an integrated information service 'which is responsive, cost-effective and appropriate to user needs and which is capable of developing and responding to changing needs and technology' (Aberystwyth Information Service, 1995) seemed a step in the right direction. However, despite an obvious awareness of how the worlds of information, technology and communications were converging and how a more integrated service might provide useful strategic leadership in this area it is difficult to resist the conclusion that the University's decision was essentially an opportunistic one resulting from a coincidence of timing and circumstances, perhaps reinforced by a somewhat ill-defined feeling that it was time for change, an opportunity to break the mould and establish structures that would be more responsive to institutional needs well into the new century.

Model

Although the Working Party was clearly aware of the useful distinctions made in the Fielden report between different types of convergence, there is no evidence to suggest that a systematic evaluation of alternative conceptual models played a significant part in determining the ultimate shape of the converged service at UWA. On the contrary, it is clear that having taken the fundamental decision to bring University Library, Computer Unit and Audio-Visual Services Unit together within a single managerial structure, the Working Party was content to do little more than put down a few organizational markers, based on an assessment of local circumstances and priorities, which could be fleshed out in more detail later. The organizational model adopted can be best summarized by reference to the further particulars for the post of Director prepared in January 1995, which referred to the Director being responsible for 'a combined information service under a single head, with a single budget and a single strategic plan for the integrated service'.

A combined Information Service

In the case of UWA the services to be brought together under the Information Services umbrella readily identified themselves. To my knowledge no other contenders for inclusion were identified or given serious consideration. When Information Services came into existence in September 1995 I inherited a staff complement of approximately 120 full and part-time staff (one-third of whom were academic-related staff) housed in six principal locations (including four separate libraries) on three University sites and a total annual budget of just under £3 million, with both staff complements and budgets being previously divided in a roughly 2:1 ratio in favour of the University Library.

A single head

No job description was prepared for the new post beyond a bland reference in the further particulars to responsibility 'for the management and operation of an integrated information service' and a statement that 'it will be an early priority of the newly appointed Director to prepare a strategic plan and management structure for the integrated service for approval by the College'. However, it is clear that the original Working Party was persuaded by the strategic, managerial and service arguments in favour of creating a single central service and that it expected that the Director would have a critical role to play not only in releasing that potential for the benefit of users but also in providing the University with a holistic view of its information needs and future information strategy. Provision was made for the new Director to report direct to the Vice-Chancellor and to play a part in the management and planning processes of the institution through ex officio membership of various bodies, including Senate and the Academic Affairs Committee, the principal focus for quality assurance and academic issues within the institution. There was no provision, however, for the Director of Information Services to join the University Planning Group, the University's small senior management team.

A single budget

Arrangements were made for Information Services to receive a single annual budget allocation of over 10% of total University disposable income, combining the 6% previously received by the University Library, the 3% received by the Computer Unit and an additional amount for Audio-Visual Services. It was expected that a single allocation, with associated responsibility for how it should be deployed, would enable the Director to take a much more strategic approach to the deployment of resources than hitherto and encourage a more effective use of scarce resources. Although provision was subsequently made for an Information Services Committee to scrutinize and approve budgetary estimates, in reality the Director was granted wide discretion over the shape and complexion of the budget and the relative priorities to be attached to often competing demands on limited budget resources.

A single strategic plan

In conformity with the view that convergence provided the University with an opportunity to align the planning, resourcing and delivery of information services more closely with institutional priorities, particular emphasis was initially placed on the need to create a single strategic plan for the newly converged service. In the event, the strategic planning process that occupied centre stage during the early months of the new organization's existence proved invaluable, not only as a means of providing Information Services with a clear sense of purpose, direction and identity, but also as a means of managing change and accelerating the integration process by bringing Information Services staff together, often for the first time, to work in concert on common issues and joint initiatives.

Structure

Apart from defining the four characteristics outlined above the University provided no steer on organizational structures or on the extent to which organizational change should lead to operational convergence. Having favoured the appointment of an executive director with full managerial responsibilities reporting directly to the Vice-Chancellor it seemed logical to give the Director discretion to make plans and bring forward proposals for consideration. Although there were pressures from within to introduce a new structure at the earliest opportunity a conscious decision was made to delay structural change until the process could be informed by the outcomes of the strategic planning exercise and until the Director could form his own opinions on the need for change from wide-ranging consultations with staff, users and University officers. The key messages that emerged from this consultative process were that any new structure should, as far as possible:

- be service oriented
- preserve and build on the strength of existing structures
- be organic and able to adapt to new opportunities and circumstances
- recognize and respect the different professional skills, expertise and experience of its staff
- have a distinctive public profile and a corporate identity which provokes a strong sense of allegiance among its staff.

Although some institutions have favoured a 'big bang' approach to staff restructuring this was not the preferred option at UWA. In order to build on perceived strengths, maintain a degree of continuity and retain staff allegiance a more incremental approach was adopted. The new structure introduced in January 1997 consisted of a mixture of old and new, with most of the six new divisions into which Information Services was divided having obvious origins in previous departments or sections but with several being either completely new groupings of staff drawn from all three previously separate services (such as the Learning Technology and Media Services Division) or subsuming some functions and staff from both University Library and Computer Unit (such as the Library and Advisory Services Division). A new post of Deputy Director was created and six posts of Assistant Director to manage the divisions, which were themselves divided into functional teams, each headed by a nominated team leader. The Director, Deputy Director and the six Assistant Directors formed the senior management team and various horizontal committees and working groups were established to facilitate cross-divisional and inter-team working.

Impact

Institutional strategy

The opportunities presented by convergence for taking a holistic view of the institution's information needs and developing information strategies that closely match institutional objectives were particularly appealing to the senior University officers who took the decision to opt for convergence. The creation of a large, multifaceted central service with wide-ranging responsibilities for information management under the direction of a single Director expected to play an active part in University affairs has strengthened accountability, raised the profile of Information Services and given it a higher level of entry into institutional affairs. A concrete example of the elevated standing associated with the converged service is the fact that the Information Services Committee is chaired by the Vice-Chancellor and includes in its membership the Registrar, the Academic Registrar, the pro-vice-chancellors and the deans, while the separate committees it replaced were chaired by a pro-vice-chancellor and mainly comprised senior academic representatives. Moreover, the breadth of knowledge and expertise now available within the single organization has given Information Services the opportunity to take an institutional leadership role in developing areas where previously several services would have been involved. Examples include the development of corporate web services; the promotion and support of learning technologies, including first computer-assisted learning and latterly virtual learning environments; the development of management information services and of compliance regimes for such matters as data protection, copyright, freedom of information, computer law and records management.

Policy and planning

At a departmental level the sheer breadth of the Information Services remit provides an opportunity to develop a holistic approach to information and knowledge management, to draw the big picture and to add the finer operational detail within a departmental setting, thereby avoiding many of the problems of territory, authority and funding often associated with inter-departmental projects and initiatives. Decision-making and priority setting is informed by a multi-annual strategic plan to guide Information Services as a whole, supported at a divisional level by annual operational plans, with the principal co-ordinating role for policy and planning being adopted by the Senior Management Group meeting on a regular three week cycle. However, although the wider remit reduces the need to develop policy across departmental boundaries the same characteristic can also complicate and slow down internal policy and decision-making. By comparison with non-converged services there are often more issues and ramifications to be considered, more people to be involved in the discussion and decision-making, more potentially conflicting interests to be resolved. Just as policy-making is complicated by the sheer breadth of interests that need to be taken into account, so too is decision-making at an operational level less straightforward than in pre-merger days because of the concerns about conforming to or avoiding conflict with policies in operation elsewhere in the organization, or about setting precedents that might compromise activities elsewhere.

Resource management

Information Services receives a genuinely single budget allocation, with the Director, in consultation with the Deputy Director, enjoying considerable scope to use his discretion and professional judgement in the deployment of resources. Budget proposals, financial estimates and expenditure returns are made to the Information Services Committee but on no occasion so far has the Committee chosen to vary proposals in any significant way. Although it goes without saying that a high proportion of the annual budget allocation is already committed in respect of staff salaries, journal subscriptions, software licences, maintenance contracts, and so on, financial flexibility, the ability to move resources around in the light of changing strategic objectives, is one of the particular strengths and most enduring attractions of convergence at UWA. As a consequence, at various stages during the past nine years Information Services has been able to divert funds into large-scale projects directly associated with the achievement of wider strategic objectives. Recent examples include rolling programmes to provide PC-based data projection facilities in all teaching rooms, network connections in halls of residence and electronic library resources.

The critical mass produced by the converged service has also provided opportunities for economies of scale and for resource sharing, particularly at the intersection between previously separate library, computing and audiovisual services. However, convergence is not a panacea for inadequate financial support; joined up budgets do not magically create more resources and, in my experience, large single budgets do not necessarily provide more clout or attract additional funds. Indeed, when times are tough at an institutional level the sheer size of the budget can sometimes attract unwanted attention and even raiding parties; in less dramatic times the 'you have such a large budget that you must be able to afford to . . .' syndrome also occasionally comes to the fore. And it goes without saying that as new technologies mature and new applications come on stream so the territory to be covered expands faster than the size of the budget itself!

Services

Although there is no doubt that the range and quality of services enjoyed by staff and students today are significantly better than in 1995 it is difficult to determine how much of this is down to convergence and how much would have happened anyway. In terms of resource provision the corporate support given to Information Services during its 'honeymoon' period certainly helped to secure very large additional resource allocations for such things as a major refurbishment of the Hugh Owen Library and for upgrading the IT infrastructure, and continuing goodwill has undoubtedly helped when institutional financial fortunes have taken a tumble. More generally, the combined resources and expertise of the converged department have provided a richer and more varied resource base from which to deliver high quality services to the staff and students of the University. Some services have been integrated (for instance help desk and advisory services, teaching room and workstation room support, study skills programmes); others have been created to support new developments in areas like learning technology and electronic information and yet more have been made more convenient and accessible through the use of multiple access points (purchase of consumables, print quota, course bookings, and so on). Arguably more significant than these visible changes have been the general improvements in standards and quality that have resulted from having a better-trained workforce. This provides greater and more diverse access to in-house expertise, knowledge and back-up, particularly in the use of IT, than would have been available in a non-converged situation.

Observations

Convergence is not one of those matters that reaches the top of the agenda, demands immediate attention and then disappears as the next urgent issue takes its place. It may well recede into the background once the dust has settled on the initial formative period but thereafter it provides a constant organizational backdrop against which to define the future development and work of the organization. Use of the label 'convergence' may well gradually disappear from the professional vocabulary but its consequences continue to manifest themselves in many different ways. For instance, convergence inevitably leads to larger, more complex organizational units. While increased size and presence has been beneficial at UWA in areas noted in the previous section, it has also complicated decision-making, placed considerable strains on internal channels of communication and consultation processes and tended to encourage a more bureaucratic approach to the management of staff and resources. The sheer scope and ever expanding nature of the remit has also placed great strain on the ability of staff to control their workloads (and stress levels) and to keep pace with technological change, a problem exacerbated at UWA by static or declining resource levels. And the tendency to create more amorphous organizational units in order to accommodate a wider range of interests can sometimes lead to a loss of identity and focus, which can in turn lead to difficulties in respect of liaison and contact with service users.

Much has been made of the clash of professional cultures that convergence brings into sharp focus and the real constraints on delivering common agendas imposed by the very different personality and behavioural traits assigned to librarians and computer specialists. Although there have been occasions when stereotypical differences of attitude and approach have shown through in Aberystwyth these have mostly resulted, in my view, from misunderstandings or the kind of one-off personality clashes that happen in any large organization rather than because of any innate incompatibility between constituent groups in the converged service. By far the biggest practical constraint on integration at an operational level and on convergence as a 'state of mind' at UWA has been the fact that staff continue to be dispersed across six buildings on three different University sites. Although the Senior Management Group works effectively as a single coherent unit, lower down the hierarchy the lack of physical convergence constitutes a real barriers to informal communication, operational synergy and social interaction. Although managerial measures have been taken to alleviate barriers to horizontal interaction and communication, such as the creation of a series of cross divisional advisory groups, the reality is that integration cannot be taken much further until and unless staff have the opportunity to work alongside each other on a continuous, day-to-day basis.

There was a danger in the mid to late 1990s that convergence would become an end in itself, with various macho versions of the concept being hailed as the models to which all self-respecting institutions should aspire. Today, it is possible to take a more balanced view of convergence as merely a means to an end, one of various ways in which institutions can manage their resources effectively and provide their clientele with high quality information services. I happen to think that convergence as defined at UWA has, by and large, worked well and more than justified its introduction – but I would say that, wouldn't I!

Structures have been adapted to meet changing circumstances – including a reduction of divisions from six to five at a time when the University was going through a particularly bad financial patch – but the fundamental concept has not been challenged. Despite that, I would not go as far as to say that what suits Aberystwyth would be ideal elsewhere or, indeed, that the present configuration will always necessarily represent the best solution for Aberystwyth. The model will continue to evolve and be refined as circumstances change, with the well known catch-phrase 'think global, act local' as perhaps a useful pointer if Information Services grows larger and becomes more diffuse. No doubt there will be a pause for stock-taking when it is time to appoint the next Director, although I suspect that, as in 1995, politics and personalities will play as big a part as track record in determining the future shape of Information Services.

References

Aberystwyth Information Services (1995) UWA internal document.

John Fielden Consultancy (1993) *Supporting Expansion: a report on human resource management in academic libraries for the Joint Funding Councils' Libraries Review Group*, Bristol, HEFCE.

Joint Funding Councils' Libraries Review Group (1993) *Report* (the Follett Report), Bristol, HEFCE.

4

A decade of convergence: information services at the University of Birmingham

Michele Shoebridge

The University of Birmingham was the first UK Russell Group (an association of 19 major research-intensive universities in the UK) university to adopt a converged model for its academic information services. The process has been well documented (Field, 1996, 1999) but this case study aims to re-visit the process, review why and how the service has evolved since 1995, assess the strengths and weaknesses of the converged model and try to predict where things may be going in the future.

The University

Established in 1900, Birmingham was one of the first redbrick universities. A century on the University now has 20 academic schools undertaking teaching and research across a wide spectrum of disciplines in arts, humanities, social sciences, physical and life sciences, engineering, medicine and law. Although Birmingham sees itself primarily as a research-led University, submitting in 49 individual areas in the 2001 Research Assessment Exercise and achieving 5 or 5* in 32 individual categories, teaching is obviously very important and extends across a very broad range of disciplines, covering 34 of the 42 Quality Assurance Agency (QAA) subject areas.

The University has around 6000 staff and some 25,000 students, of whom over 30% are postgraduate. Following a merger with a local college of higher education the University now operates on two campuses, the main one in Edgbaston and a smaller one in Selly Oak. The Birmingham College of Food, Tourism and Creative Studies is the only accredited college of the University, with nearly 3000 students of whom some 2000 are working towards degrees or other qualifications of the University.

The University's administration or Corporate Services is headed by the Registrar and Secretary and comprises Finance, Personnel, Academic Office, Estates, Hospitality, Research and Enterprise, Public Relations, Development & Alumni Relations, Information Services and the Legal Office. Information Services, with a staff of around 450 bodies operating across 17 sites and with a total budget of around £16 million, is one of the largest offices within the Corporate Services.

Background to convergence

The decision to converge at Birmingham was very much an executive decision that emerged after the publication of the Follett report (Joint Funding Councils' Library Review Group) in 1993. The University's Strategy, Planning and Resources Committee steered the process through an Information Services working party made up of senior members of the University – including the Vice Principal, Pro-Vice-Chancellor for Teaching and Learning, Registrar and Secretary and senior academics. Their remit was: 'In the light of the Follett report and the changing needs of the University for effectiveness and efficiency in its information, teaching and learning support services to consider . . . those services over the next decade . . .'

Although it was a top down decision, the indication from the Librarian at the time that he would retire in 1995 made it easier to move in a new direction. The process itself was a fairly long one starting with desk research, moving on to informal soundings about the effectiveness of the providers of academic information services and then more formal written evidence from four actual providers and the Guild of Students. No external consultants or advisors were used and there were no study trips to see at first hand how convergence was working in North America! All the recommendations were presented at the University's Senate but there was very little debate there.

The key objectives, many of which are just as relevant today, were:

- to maximize the potential of communications and IT (C&IT)
- to facilitate the transition from teaching to learning
- to encourage generic skills among students
- to heighten the information skills of academic staff
- to eliminate the functional overlap between service providers
- to address some problems in the management structures
- to optimize resources at a time of declining funding.

The model in 1995

There was an early decision that any converged service would include the University Library (dating back to 1875 and comprising a large central library and ten site libraries), the Academic Computing Service (which had emerged from a centre for computing and computer science), Television Services (the production arm of an audiovisual unit) and the Centre for Computer Based Learning (a focus for computer-assisted learning (CAL) activities). The combined resources at that time were over 200 full-time equivalent staff and direct and indirect expenditure of around £9 million. The name adopted for the service was Information Services and the head of service title became 'Librarian and Director' reporting directly to the Registrar and Secretary.

The model that was adopted was a radical functional one, which necessitated dissolving existing library, computing and media structures and grouping future activity around five 'divisions', each to be led by an Assistant Director. These divisions were: Collection Management (including Special Collections), Information and Computing Systems, Learning and Research Support, Planning and Administration and Public Services.

Major challenges in getting the new structure working revolved around cultural issues, harmonizing working practices and procedures for the assimilation of staff. There were published guidelines for the assimilation. Half the available academic posts in the new structure were filled by a designation process following expressions of interest, the other half were filled by open competition. There were a number of early retirements, severances and staff designated to posts at a lower grade, so generally this was a painful time for many staff. Assimilating the support staff was not so difficult because although line management arrangements had often changed the content had not, the exception being some of the computing posts. The relevant trade unions were involved throughout the entire process, which took almost a year and consumed a lot of energy.

Once the service was up and running a number of other activities were integrated into the new structure. The management of the language teaching laboratories was merged into a new language and media resource centre and site library within the Public Services Division. A new Learning Resources Accommodation Team was created to provide support for the design, maintenance and teaching equipment in all centrally managed lecture theatres and seminar rooms. It was located in the Learning and Research Support Division to ensure that developments in teaching space mirrored changes in the pedagogic process. A new venture, the University of Birmingham Press, set up to co-ordinate and promote academic publishing, was also located in the Learning and Research Support Division. In a major change in 1999, which recognized the need to bring all aspects of computing under one umbrella, administrative computing was integrated into Information Services as a totally separate division – Corporate Information Services – which was also responsible for the infrastructure of the University website. This exploited the synergies between web delivery and the corporate data systems. Finally, the University's Central Printing Service, a self-financing operation, was trans-ferred into the Public Services Division to sit alongside the existing repro-graphics operation in Information Services. Additional work occurred in 1999 when the University merged with Westhill College of Higher Education and Information Services took over responsibility for its central learning centre.

There was no formal change process around convergence as such and certainly no external consultants to help with some of the difficult problems like reconciling the different professional backgrounds. So, no bottom-up consultation, focus groups, newsletters, and so on. The objectives that were set at the beginning were legitimate but difficult to measure as success criteria. Staff development and communication policies, considered to be important to bring about cultural change, were developed but with too much emphasis on 'process' and not enough on actual delivery or success in getting staff to take ownership of what had emerged. There was no 'mourning' of the passing of some of the old cultural icons that were swept away with convergence or celebration of new things that emerged. Despite this it was a success and all credit is due to the Director and the senior management team for having the vision to create one of the most integrated and stable services in the UK, so much so that when academic staff at Birmingham were canvassed about the converged service in 2001 they were positive and indicated that they wanted it to continue as a converged service.

A decade on . . .

It is now almost ten years since Information Services was created and five since the last service was integrated. Much has been achieved and the service is understood and well regarded by academics and students. However, there is always room for improvement and in 2002 a change programme was created to assist in the realignment of the mission and objectives to fit more closely with those of the University, to respond to new challenges and to tackle some of the cultural issues that inevitably still existed. The challenges included the diversification of the student base; plans for the introduction of student fees and more demanding students; the move to 'personalization' of services be it for research or learning; the increasing importance of the C&IT structure, particularly the network, to the business continuity of the University; the huge increase in the web for accessing information and in the use of virtual learning

environments for delivering teaching; the changes in scholarly commun-
ications, the emphasis on activity-based costing and compliance; and the
University's decision that the Corporate Services should seek to get Investors in
People accreditation.

An external consultant was engaged to provide support for the process and
senior staff attended a change management course. The Registrar and Secretary
took the role of sponsor and a formal change team was established. A regular
newsletter was issued and a website set up to provide a two-way communication channel. The mission statement was updated putting emphasis on the
customer:

> Information Services enhances the learning, teaching, research and management of
> the University through:
>
> • delivering a reliable and efficient service
> • continuing to improve our services through innovation and collaboration
> • anticipating and responding to customers' needs
> • fostering a culture of creativity by developing and empowering staff
> • being outward looking and a beacon of good practice institutionally, regionally,
>   nationally and internationally
> • being positive and supportive influence on the University's mission.

Many of the success criteria involved staff embracing change, for example staff
moving from 'declining' areas to new, emerging areas, often 'moving out of the
closet onto the stage' (cataloguers becoming learning advisors; staff adopting
different ways of working by supplementing face-to-face contact with web
delivery whether it be skills training, enquiries, book issues or creating learning
materials). Dedicated e-learning, customer IT support and quality teams were
created and the academic support teams expanded.

Other objectives involved developing more effective and transparent
communication channels within IS and creating an effective and vibrant
middle manager cohort with a reduction in the number of issues being bounced
up to the senior management team.

The new structure in 2004

As a result of the change programme there was an extensive re-structuring
exercise, in which the number of divisions was reduced from six to four. Over
40 posts were disestablished and new posts created. The work undertaken by
the Collection Management Division had changed considerably – primarily
because of the easy availability of catalogue records, changes in research

publishing and the general increase in the number of electronic resources. Manuscripts and Archives were no longer just about 'collections' but more about embedding them in the research and learning and teaching. Consequently Bibliographic Services and Special Collections were moved into the Learning and Research Support Division. Some professional cataloguers secured new posts in the academic support teams and received appropriate re-skilling, for example in delivering face-to-face training, developing learning materials and one opted to be re-trained as an archivist. A new acquisition and metadata support team, comprising mainly para-professionals, was set up to process materials and support the academic support teams whose only ongoing involvement in the cataloguing process is checking classification. The bindery and the university press were moved to Public Services to sit alongside printing and reprographics to form a nucleus of income generating activities. Support for teaching rooms also moved into Public Services in recognition that it is firmly a customer-facing activity.

In line with many other universities, administrative and academic computing were finally merged into one division to reflect the technology transfer and their mutual dependency. Although a relatively new initiative and despite bringing two different IT cultures together it has worked well at both the strategic and operational level and is delivering real benefits in a more joined up approach to delivering services and interacting with the customers.

Benefits of convergence

The converged structure is constantly changing and will continue to do so. A recent review of the Information Services change programme and resulting structure found much to be positive about and acknowledged real benefits in the converged model. At a strategic level it can be very useful having one post responsible for learner support, C&IT and teaching accommodation both in visionary and in 'making it happen' terms. This is particularly true of small to medium sized institutions and works effectively in larger institutions if there is enough staff resource in place. Possible exceptions are those universities where the remit is just too big, for instance where there are extremely prestigious archive collections and/or national computing services.

Two obvious examples of convergence working well at Birmingham are the portal and the virtual learning environment (VLE). The my.bham portal project was managed by the Portal/Corporate Web Team but required input from technical infrastructure staff and staff from business systems web enabling the student record system, the digital library, room bookings and the VLE to populate the portal software and Help Desk staff to support the roll out. Significantly that project also involved working closely with staff in the

Academic Office who had to re-engineer their business processes. Similarly our early adoption of an institutional VLE – WebCT – and its high take-up has been achieved by a joined approach between technical, applications, pedagogic and bibliographic staff across three different divisions of Information Services. The eLearning pedagogy has had a real impact on learning spaces and led to a more creative approach at Birmingham. Obviously all these things can be, and are, achieved in a non-converged service but anecdotal evidence suggests it is much easier in a converged model.

As the Information Services change programme has shown, it can be easier to re-direct resources in a converged model, and this is particularly useful given the challenging times ahead for libraries, academic support and C&IT services. Obviously 're-balancing' should not be done arbitrarily but at the end of the day the majority of most IS budgets is spent on staff so it is essential that staff are valued and developed but deployed in areas that support the institution's needs. Mentoring, coaching, influencing, performance management, change and project management are going to be equally, if not more, important than technical or professional knowledge and experience, and one of the biggest threats is that staff cannot or will not adapt to the new culture that is required. This is not to say that technical and professional knowledge is not important but as information services-type activity becomes ever more critical and universities become big businesses there will be a greater need to draw on external advice – via management consultants, IT analysts and so on – to supplement internal staff.

The qualities required of heads of converged services must include good management skills and not having a strong allegiance to any one part of the service. There are many dangers to fall into: getting bogged down in the detail and complexity of the service to the detriment of strategic planning and leadership, failing to convince staff in any particular areas that their 'area' will still have a voice, failing to convince staff that they work in a fast changing environment and they must change, and failing to get the confidence of line managers, senior academics and others in the converged model. Although somewhat dated now the HIMSS (Hybrid Information Management: Skills for Senior Staff, see www.himss.bham.ac.uk) project report contains some useful material about the qualities required by Directors (Lancaster and Dalton, 2003).

Conclusion

A successful converged Information Services model can provide a sound building block in an important challenge now being faced by many of the older universities – getting a more 'joined up' approach across all their 'corporate' services to provide customized information and services to users from cradle to grave via personalized interfaces like portals and one stop shops. As for the argument for and against converged library and IT, most users of the services, be they academic staff, researchers or particularly students, do not really care who does what as long as the service is friendly, efficient and transparent. Technology, process re-engineering and the ability of staff to adapt to a changing environment across traditional boundaries will be the key to delivering this.

References

Field, C.D. (1996) Implementing convergence at the University of Birmingham, *SCONUL Newsletter*, **9**, Winter, 33–7.

Field, C.D. (1999) Carry on Converging: the continued implementation of convergence at the University of Birmingham, *SCONUL Newsletter*, **17**, Summer/Autumn, 19–25.

Joint Funding Councils' Libraries Review Group (1993) *Report* (the Follett Report), Bristol, HEFCE.

Lancaster, K and Dalton, P. (2003) Recruitment, Training and Succession Planning in the HE sector: findings from the HIMSS project, Birmingham, the University of Birmingham.

5

From two Brighton Piers to one: convergence at the University of Brighton

Mark Toole

The University of Brighton was formed in 1992 from Brighton Polytechnic, which itself was founded in 1970 with the amalgamation of Brighton Colleges of Technology and Art and Design and later incorporated the Brighton College of Education and the East Sussex College of Higher Education. In 1994 the Sussex and Kent Institute of Nursing and Midwifery joined the University. The Brighton and Sussex Medical School (BSMS) was opened in 2003, a joint venture with the University of Sussex and local NHS Trusts. The institution has a strong multi-site character, chiefly operating from three main sites in Brighton, its site in Eastbourne and managing the new University Centre, Hastings.

The University has an emphasis on providing professional and vocational education with currently around 17,800 enrolled students (12,500 FTEs, 3000 taught postgraduates, 350 research postgraduates). Academic coverage is wide; currently there are five faculties (Arts and Architecture; Science & Engineering; Management and Information Sciences; Education & Sport; Health).

The winding road to convergence

The University of Brighton (and as Brighton Polytechnic) has a long history of multi-professional support teams. For example, by the mid 1990s the Learning Resources department consisted of: libraries, media production (then one of the largest in the UK), reprographics and graphics design. The Computer Centre contained within its remit general computing to support academic programmes, administrative computing (MIS) and the management of the University Computer Store. As a result, years of experience had been accrued in co-ordinating different professional cultures in support services in an institutional environment with a history of integrating different academic cultures.

It is therefore no surprise that at this time the University was considering bringing both these departments together. A review group was formed consisting of the Deputy Director of the University (himself a former Head of Learning Resources); representatives of Learning Resources and the Computer Centre; and academic colleagues with expertise in information sciences. The group examined the potential benefits for the University and scrutinized other institutions with converged services. It was concluded that there were merits in establishing a converged organization, but that it was not the right time to do this at Brighton.

In 2000 when the Head of Learning Resources was promoted to a senior management post, it was decided to re-visit the work of the convergence group. This further review was once again led by the University's Deputy Director. This time the review concluded that the time was ripe for the establishment of a multi-professional converged service at the University. The two main reasons for the change of view were the increasing pace of deployment of electronic information services and the increasing importance of supporting the use of learning technology.

Following a period of an approach of 'let a thousand flowers bloom' to the introduction of learning technology, the University had concluded by 2000 that the best way forward to sustain the progress made so far was to centralize the development and support of learning technology. Such a service would straddle the activities of many departments. It was agreed that this new service would be best located with staff then working in Learning Resources and Computer Centre. Another component of the nascent department was coming into place.

A proposal was prepared and this included the following principal drivers for the new structure:

- the desire to exploit the key strengths of the departments to provide a more coherent and seamless set of information services
- awareness that the availability of more information services in electronic format requires both information skills and ICT skills in order to develop, deliver and support those services effectively
- awareness that the development of intranets to support learning, teaching, research and administration requires the use of technology-based skills and information (design and handling) organization skills in order to develop, deliver and support those services

- awareness that the development, delivery and support of learning technologies requires technical skills, subject knowledge and the ability to integrate appropriate applications and appropriate information
- recognition that information seeking, handling and ICT skills training would be better co-ordinated as a coherent programme as they are interdependent
- recognition that convergence of some aspects of media services with ICT services such as streaming video services over a network requires multiple skills and coherent planning to develop and deliver those emerging services effectively
- recognition that convergence of technologies and skills sets offers an opportunity to change the way in which services are offered and supported.

Information Services at the University of Brighton was thus born following a decision of the Board of Governors on 5 May 2000.

Change management: developing an organizational and operational model for Information Services

An implementation group was formed consisting of the management teams of Learning Resources and the Computer Centre once the creation of Information Services had been agreed.

This group undertook an initial analysis of the strengths and weaknesses of the departments following briefing sessions, which enabled members to become familiar with the services delivered by, and the structure of, each department. Informed by this analysis, and other factors such as the principal drivers behind the merger and prevailing University policies and strategies, a number of specific, initial objectives for the new department were drawn up. Some research was also carried out by the group into the structures of converged library and computing services elsewhere. It was noted that many 'so-called merged services' were actually run as separate services under a single director; when services were more truly merged the 'user services' aspects were managed under one umbrella. Little evidence was found of 'hybrid' support staff, with the distinctions between information and ICT support staff remaining.

The group concluded that in, order to achieve the initial objectives, a model of retaining two separate departments under one director would not be the best choice, as 'it would not promote better planning, co-ordination and delivery of library, media and computing services'.

Members of the group and others in the department submitted proposals for a new structure. After examining these, the Head and Deputy Head of

Information Services devised a number of options for evaluation by the group as a whole; eventually a revised organizational structure and definition of roles were agreed. During the summer and autumn of 2000 the proposals were discussed in detail with staff on all sites: it was noted in a Committee report of this consultation process that 'no major concerns with the proposed management structure were raised other than concerns about how liaison between sections will be achieved'.

The revised structure was implemented from the autumn of 2000 to September 2001. Some existing sections (such as Administrative Computing and Network Services) changed little. The User Services Group of the Computer Centre was disbanded, with some staff being absorbed into the library organization and some others re-located into an expanded Desktop Systems group (which now became responsible for both hardware and first line of software support for staff and students). A new post was created, 'network information manager', responsible for the co-ordination of the procurement, promotion and development of electronic resources (applications software and electronic information such as e-journals, databases etc); Library Technical Services (main activities, book purchasing and support of the library management system); and Library Media Services.

'Information service managers' were appointed for each of the major sites with a remit to develop a detailed knowledge and understanding of the academic work carried out on the site to enable them to formulate Information Services' policy for the site and determine priorities for services on that site. They are also responsible for the day-to-day operation of the library and media services on that site, but the day-to-day supervision of the operation of frontline computing services on all sites is under the remit of Desktop Systems to ensure that there is a consistency of ICT technical support services across the University.

The implementation group has subsequently evolved into the Information Services Group (ISG), which today is the management group of the department; this takes overall responsibility for the planning and co-ordination of all the services across the department and is the main decision-making group within Information Services.

Essentially, the Brighton model is one of management convergence with some service integration in certain areas. The presence of media and learning technology services is interwoven into many aspects of the department. The organization of the department, and the services it offers, is strongly influenced by the multi-site nature of the University, where there is no one 'central site' but four major sites of significant academic activity: the Information Services staff at each site are expected to offer a common baseline set of services, augmented by services that are tailored for the specific characteristics of the site.

Once the decision in principle to proceed with convergence had been taken, the implementation was handled by the department, with advice and monitoring from the University's committee structure and management.

Information Services at the University of Brighton

As at July 2004, there are just over 200 members of staff in Information Services, on six sites in Brighton and East Sussex. The budget for 2004–5 is £8.3 million (which represents 8.6% of the total University budget). The department is responsible for services across the University, in the BSMS (where the University takes the lead in student services) and in the University Centre, Hastings. These services include: library; computing; learning technology, including leading the development of the University's emerging managed learning environment (MLE) and the staff intranet; graphic design; media production; audio-visual; reprographics; and the Computer Store.

Evaluating the experience so far

The first formal evaluation of the new arrangements was made by a new Director of Information Services following his arrival in spring 2002. Evidence was collected by one-to-one interviews with over 30 members of the department and 25 key stakeholders in the University. The principal evaluation criteria were: progress in achieving the initial objectives set at the time of merger; alignment of activities with prevailing strategies and policies of the University; and levels of service compared with other information services in the sector.

The main output of the evaluation was a SWOT (strengths, weaknesses, opportunities, threats) analysis. This concluded that broadly the new organization was functioning well; good progress was being made on most of the initial objectives; the services to the University were generally good and well appreciated; and most Information Services staff identified themselves with the new department.

The analysis identified a weakness in long-term planning; in particular the initial objectives were seen as being too narrowly focused and gave no clear sense of the direction. Consequently, an Information Services Strategy 2002–7 was developed. Fortuitously, the corporate plan was being revised at the same time and the University's Learning and Teaching Strategy had also been recently revised, thereby allowing a good opportunity to strongly align the new Information Services Strategy with these. A key element of the new strategy is a 'vision' statement to try and articulate to members of the department, and the University community, the impact on the activities of the University that is expected to result from planned service development. The strategy has

16 principal aims; interestingly, only four of these can be considered to be solely in the realm of 'library' or 'computing'.

Another finding of the SWOT analysis was that the re-location of some members of the old Computer Centre User Services to work alongside library colleagues had not been successful. In hindsight their new roles were over-ambitious and too wide ranging; some aspects of their role were being overtaken by events, principally the changing nature of support for academic colleagues caused by the deployment of the MLE. Consequently, it was agreed to re-focus these roles to direct support for the MLE as part of the department's Learning Technologies Group in the department. Their relatively brief spell working alongside library colleagues did, however, accrue two major benefits: a significant improvement of the ICT skills of many of the library staff; and establishment of excellent working relationships that have proved to be of lasting benefit in providing holistic support for the MLE.

The operation of the department is formally evaluated annually when ISG considers progress against the annual departmental operating plan (derived directly from the Information Services Strategy) and changes to the departmental risk register, and when the Learning Resources Committee considers the department's annual report. While the early signs are encouraging, it is recognized that the high value benefits to the University of the new arrangements are not likely to accrue for five years at least. So it is planned to conduct a richer evaluation of progress with significant involvement by the user community and integrated into the initial work for revising the Information Services Strategy.

Additional objective evidence for the progress of the new arrangements is difficult to obtain, but the consistent praise for the services of the department in internal subject reviews and in professional and statutory body accreditation reviews by external agencies bears testament to a high degree of satisfaction with the work of the department. The recent QAA Institutional Audit also indicated that the department is operating well; two out of the seven 'examples of good practice' in the institution cited by the auditors were for activities undertaken by the department.

Benefits so far

At this relatively early stage the University has had several 'quick wins'. First, the availability within the department of a wide range of multi-professional skills and experience has been a significant factor in the successful and highly effective role it has played in the implementation of a number of major new high profile University initiatives. These include the deployment of the MLE; the launch of University Centre, Hastings; and the opening of BSMS. All have been substantial projects requiring cohesive, and in some cases integrated, library and computing services developed on tight timescales, with multiple stakeholders and often with complex technical or organizational requirements.

Second, partly because of the location of support staff across so many campuses, there have been real operational benefits of bringing together small groups of staff in a co-ordinated and co-operative environment, such as providing better resilience, back-up and efficiency. One example is that now all centrally managed student workstations, whether in the open access computer rooms, teaching rooms or in the libraries, are set-up and managed by Desktop Systems. This has resulted in more consistent and reliable services for the students, a higher level of efficiency in the management of these systems and a more co-ordinated upgrade programme. As a second example, in autumn 2004 there were severe network connectivity problems to the Eastbourne campus for several weeks; one result of this was that many students were unable to establish their computer accounts. Staff in the Eastbourne library individually activated students' computer accounts and coached students to use the systems in a way that minimized the effect of the network disruption, enabling technicians to concentrate on solving the problem and assisting staff in accessing key systems to ensure business continuity at a particularly busy time of year.

Third, ISG has proved to be an excellent body for taking the lead in the development of information facilities and services at the University. A case where truly 'the sum is greater than the parts'. Even when topics are being discussed that are almost entirely about 'library' or 'computing', contributions from those whose main area of responsibility or expertise is elsewhere are often illuminating or open up new ways of thinking about a problem or implications for the University community. It has also enabled the University to undertake activities requiring multi-professional skills more easily, such as the Information Architecture Task Force whose work has provided coherence to the different web-based services that were previously developing in an uncoordinated manner across the University.

Discussion: transferable and non-transferable lessons

Some obvious points first. There is no 'one size' fits all model for the organization of library and computing services at an institution. No organizational structures are set in stone; circumstances are always likely to change, which will cause the revision of structures and these affect converged or non-converged departments alike. 'Convergence' also does not just mean the coming together of computing and library services; new relationships that span traditional professional boundaries with other support services are in many cases just as important, in particular the emerging new support requirements for learning technology and digital multimedia services.

The Brighton experience is that the process of developing convergence is being eased by building on some specific characteristics of the University (such as its multi-sites and its tradition of integrating staff from different academic and professional cultures), which have lowered initial barriers to this type of change. These, of course, cannot be transferred as useful lessons to other institutions. However, there are five actions that have worked well for us which may be applicable in other environments:

- Before embarking on convergence, the drivers for change were articulated and focused on the long term; adopting convergence as a short term 'fix', for example to reduce expenditure in the light of financial pressure, seems to us a weak foundation upon which to build.
- We selected the right time to start.
- We developed a cohesive departmental management group to provide leadership that appeals to all sections of the department but takes a holistic approach to the services we offer.
- We recognized that there is no road map to successful integration of services; we knew mistakes would be made, so we put robust early warning mechanisms in place to identify them as soon as possible and then we had the courage to adjust plans and operations accordingly.
- We treat managing convergence as a change management process and therefore have used the appropriate and timely application of change management tools (such as communication, leadership, vision, values, commitment, team-building, effective planning, monitoring, evaluation and more communication).

But how vital to flourishing services are the minutiae of organizational arrangements? Successful services are fundamentally about having the right people, motivated, with the right skills and resources and who take a dynamic and holistic view of services from a user's perspective, rather than specific details of organizational structure or professional cultures. In a busy world perhaps we need the pretext of a reorganization to expend the necessary time and resources to address these issues properly.

6

Integration at the University of Bristol

Cathryn Gallacher

The University of Bristol is a research intensive, Russell Group university, which aims to retain and build on its current position as a 'world-class university'. Bristol currently has 5000 staff and 13,000 students, of whom about 20% are postgraduates. Bristol is not a campus university, and therefore its 45 academic departments and 15 research centres, arranged in six faculties, are spread around the Bristol area, with the majority of the University's buildings and activities concentrated in a square mile near the city centre.

Circumstances leading to convergence

In the first half of the 1990s, Bristol's academic support services were also widely spread both geographically and organizationally, with separate academic and administrative computing services (the latter known as the Management Information Service), a library operating on 14 sites, a small educational technology service based in the Faculty of Social Sciences and a separate Social Sciences computer unit. In the mid-1990s, however, this situation began to change when the University hired a team of external consultants to advise on educational technology. One of the consultants' recommendations resulted in the establishment of the central Institute for Learning and Research Technology (ILRT), a free-standing and largely self-funding unit. The ILRT brought together the Educational Technology Service and the Centre for Computing in the Social Sciences. The consultants' report also recommended that all academic support services be brought together under one head. In a separate development, an information strategy co-ordinator was appointed, reporting first to a pro-vice-chancellor and later to the University Librarian.

After internal discussion, the University asked the Director of the Computing Service and the University Librarian to look more closely at possibilities for collaboration, co-operation or integration of academic support services, particularly of the Library and the Computing Service. These two heads began to investigate models of convergence and collaboration used in other universities, especially those in the UK; simultaneously they organized a working group of managers from their two services to explore areas of common ground. Following this investigation, the University's Teaching and Learning Group set up a larger working party, chaired by the Dean of Social Sciences. Members of the group included senior members of academic staff as well as the two heads of support services. The report of that working party, produced in the summer of 1998, recommended that:

- the services should co-ordinate in the first instance, as a step toward later convergence
- the co-ordinated services should include the ILRT as well as the Library and the Computing Service
- one of the service heads should be appointed as co-ordinator, and that this person should produce a plan within 12 months to say which services should converge and how convergence should take place.

The report also listed several other academic support services, which might become part of a converged service. One of these was the Management Information Service (MIS).

The report of the working party was submitted to the Committee of Deans for approval and, after a lengthy period of discussion and revision, the recommendations were agreed in May 1999. In order to keep up momentum during this process, the heads of the Library, Computing Service and ILRT met regularly to co-ordinate action. Because the Head of the Computing Service was at that time heavily involved in planning for Y2K, the University Librarian was asked to chair this group.

Meanwhile, two other events taking place in the University had an impact on the speed and process of convergence. First, the University began an internal review of all support services, led by a senior member of academic staff. The subsequent report proposed significant cost savings in the Computing Service.

Second, the University Registrar retired and a successor was appointed. The new Registrar was given a larger remit which included overseeing all academic support services, previously the responsibility of a pro-vice-chancellor. When the new Registrar took up his appointment in the spring of 1999, one of his first observations was that the internal structure of support services was unwieldy and that too many people reported directly to him. He therefore proposed a more rapid convergence of the Library, Computing Service, ILRT and MIS. The Registrar asked the University Librarian to become Director of Information Services from Summer 1999, and to use the following year to amalgamate these services, and at the same time to address the University's recommendations for cost savings in computing services.

Also around the same time, the Director of the Computing Service completed the successful negotiation of Y2K and announced his retirement.

The model adopted

The integration of the services listed above took effect on 1 August 2000. The model used was based on that of the University of Birmingham, and involved significant structural integration, with redefined roles and job titles mainly at senior management level. The new Information Services was made up of six Divisions, with an Assistant Director at the head of each:

* Client Services consists of outreach, liaison and communication services. Members of the division include IT trainers and consultants, subject librarians, and other staff who are responsible for communication with users and the promotion of services. This division is also responsible for co-ordinating Information Services' various quality assurance activities, including involvement in University and departmental reviews.
* Information Management is responsible for the acquisition and dissemination of information in printed and other formats. This division includes library acquisitions, serials management, cataloguing, special collections, interlibrary loans, binding and conservation. Initially the library systems team was based in this division, but soon after integration it moved to Information Systems and Computing.
* Information Systems and Computing is responsible for managing and developing the University network and central computing services, including corporate systems and latterly library systems.
* Public Services provides library circulation, enquiry, photocopying and printing services, and oversees access to library buildings and collections and the arrangement of stock. The IT Help Desk was originally included in Public Services and steps were taken to converge this service with library enquiry services. After a year, however, the IT help desk team moved to the Information Systems and Computing division.
* The Institute for Learning and Research Technology (ILRT), which is 90% funded by external sources, carries out research, development, advice and consultancy in areas such as digital libraries, e-learning, internet design and

accessibility and the semantic web. The University-funded Learning Technology Support Service (LTSS) is part of the ILRT.

- Planning and Administrative Support has an internal focus. This division looks after finance, personnel and staff development matters for all the Information Services divisions apart from the ILRT.

In addition, the Information Strategy Co-ordinator moved to Information Services and became a member of its senior management team.

There are currently about 300 staff in Information Services. Although there has been some geographical co-location since the consolidation process began in the mid-1990s, these staff work in 16 different buildings, of which 15 are in the central University precinct.

The change management process

During the year before convergence and the launch of Information Services (IS), the Director and members of his senior staff developed the strategy and structure for the new integrated service. At the beginning of this amalgamation year, a number of internal working groups were formed, with membership from departments across the converging services. Each of these groups was given a remit to plan a particular aspect of the new service or its launch. For example, the Faculty Liaison Advisory Group (FLAG) had a remit to consult academic staff about mechanisms for ongoing liaison between faculties and IS, and to make recommendations which would inform the developing IS strategy. The strategic plan developed by these working groups and co-ordinated by the IS Director formed a key input to the budgeting process in succeeding years.

Regular communication with staff and stakeholders throughout the amalgamation year was also an important aspect of the change process. Communication with academic staff and other stakeholders was co-ordinated by a new promotion and marketing group. This group prepared print and web-based information about the new service, and oversaw the convergence of the four services' websites into a single IS web presence. This new website was introduced as part of a formal launch of Information Services.

Internal communication during the amalgamation year took a number of forms. Many staff who would become members of the converged service were not directly affected by the convergence, as neither their own roles nor those of their teams would change. There were also many staff who were not directly involved in planning or working groups. In order to ensure that those staff were informed and involved, the Director and service managers organized meetings with individual teams, as well as general staff meetings where information could be given, questions raised and concerns addressed. Additionally, an ad hoc Communication Working Group provided printed and web-based updates, including FAQs on the developing IS intranet. This group also organized 'introduction days' in which all IS staff had a chance to meet their colleagues across the service, and to talk to the new senior management team about the mission and structure of the new converged service.

Not surprisingly, however, one of the most difficult aspects of managing the change process involved the people whose roles changed considerably as a result of convergence. These people were the senior managers who had been leaders or members of management teams in the converging services. Because the structural change was significant at division level as described above, the integrated service required new posts to oversee the six new divisions. If it had been possible, the Director would have chosen to advertise all these posts externally, as had been done during convergence in other universities. However, because there was no money to accommodate existing managers if they were not successful in obtaining the new posts, this option was ruled out. Instead, decisions about appointments were made by the Director, in consultation with the University's Personnel Office, on a post-by-post basis.

The first step of this decision-making process involved defining and establishing the grade of the new Assistant Director roles. This was done using the Higher Education Role Analysis (HERA) scheme, which the University was piloting at the time. The second step was to compare the new job descriptions and grades with those of existing senior managers in the converging services. Based on this comparison, one of two things happened:

- Where the new post and an existing post were deemed to be very similar in content and at the same grade, the existing manager was appointed to the new role following brief discussion and agreement.
- Where new jobs were considered to be significantly different and/or at a higher grade than existing posts, the new jobs were advertised internally, and existing managers were invited to apply for them.

There was also one vacancy at senior management level, following the retirement of the Director of the Computing Service. Therefore, the post of Assistant Director (Information Systems and Computing) was advertised externally. An internal applicant, the former Director of MIS, was the successful candidate.

Although there were more existing managers than there were new roles, there were no redundancies, and none of the managers was left without a full or part-time role in the new senior management team. This was accomplished because those who applied for the new posts made creative use of job-sharing opportunities, and because all the managers who applied for posts were successful in obtaining them.

Taking a retrospective look at the change management process, it is possible to identify both strengths and weaknesses. On the positive side, most of the internal working groups worked well, not only accomplishing important tasks but giving their members a chance to get to know and understand each other, to identify important synergies as well as appropriate differences, and to contribute to the change process and the developing IS strategy. Additionally, the introduction days were well received by those staff who were not otherwise involved in the convergence process.

Most of the problem areas in the change management process resulted from those common university bugbears, lack of time and lack of money. If it had been possible to call on extra money earmarked for convergence, it would have been possible to change people's roles significantly without simply giving them more work and greater responsibility. If there had been longer than a year to plan and implement convergence, there would have been more time for liaison and discussion with both IS and academic staff to identify and address their issues and concerns.

As a result of the short time available to plan and implement convergence, few people apart from the Director had sufficient time to get to grips with the complexities of integrating and developing a shared strategy. Therefore, many people, both IS staff and other stakeholders, were unclear why integration was happening, and were unable to participate in its creation. Moreover, a long history of declining funds in both the Library and the Computing Service – but more stringently in the latter – engendered fears among staff that convergence was a cover for cost cutting and reduction of staffing levels. The fact that convergence was carried out hard on the heels of the Support Services Review and its recommendation to save money on computing exacerbated these fears; and when the University Librarian became the new Director (albeit with the blessing of the Director of Computing), many staff felt that convergence was in fact a 'library take-over'. Interestingly, however, many academic staff, particularly in the Arts Faculty, felt that the Library would be the service to lose out in subsequent resource prioritization.

Because of the circumstances described above, some of the working groups did not go as well as others. Differences in culture, history and understanding take time and energy to recognize and manage, and when these differences were particularly evident within a group, members found it difficult to accomplish complex tasks such as strategy development in short timescales. The difficulty was, perhaps, particularly acute for those managers who had to plan the new service while coping at the same time with major uncertainty about their own roles.

Finally, the circumstances leading to the development of the new senior management team resulted in a team with managers on two different grades. The HERA scheme, which was used to determine those grades, has since been abandoned by the University, and a new job review mechanism has not yet been implemented. Therefore the posts created at the time of convergence have not yet been reviewed. The result is a perception among team members of unresolved anomalies and status differences within the senior management team, with implications for the divisions and services they manage.

Outcomes

Two years after convergence, the Director of Information Services retired. Before the new Director was appointed there was a year's gap, during which two Assistant Directors became joint acting Directors. Because of these circumstances, IS has not yet carried out a formal evaluation of the converged structure. Nevertheless, it is possible to identify both successes and future challenges with regard to the existing structure and service.

One of the most important benefits of convergence has been the existence of a single Director and senior management team to carry out joint strategic planning and management. This shared planning has resulted in the development of ICT and Information Systems strategies which are better integrated with other University and departmental strategies. In turn these strategies have resulted in improved funding for strategic development, including funds from within the University and funds obtained through bids to HEFCE. As a result Information Services, particularly the Information Systems and Computing division, has grown in size and status since convergence.

Convergence has also increased the efficiency and effectiveness of some administrative activities. Shared functions such as the management of finance, health and safety and staff development have resulted in improved operations across the IS divisions, with benefits for the service as a whole. For example, Information Services achieved the Investors in People Award in 2003 – an outcome that would have been more difficult to attain when staff development activities were managed separately.

A number of outward facing services have also increased in efficiency and effectiveness since convergence. The University now has a centrally supported VLE, which was made possible by collaboration across IS divisions co-ordinated by a single management team. The move of the library systems team to the larger Information Systems and Computing division has resulted in shared understanding and expertise, which are passed on to users. In other areas, the existence of a single manager in charge of related though not necessarily converged functions (such as IT skills training and information skills training, for example) enables the service to take advantage of synergies, as well as to understand and defend appropriate differences. Similarly, a division with a specific remit to oversee liaison and communication with IS stakeholders helps to prevent these activities from getting lost in the delivery of more tangible and time-limited services.

There are also, inevitably, downsides to converged structures. Size alone can make communication and consultative planning more difficult, and at Bristol this situation is exacerbated by geographical spread and by the fact that, following the disbanding of the ad hoc communication group, there was for some time no specific group or individual with a strategic remit to plan and oversee internal communication.

Other areas that might also be addressed in a review of convergence at Bristol include the fact that Information Services is still perceived in the University, and largely also in the division itself, as the Library Service and the Computing Service with new and confusing names. Few people understand the structure, and there is some lack of clarity about responsibilities. In addition, while convergence has improved operations and services in some areas, the new structure has highlighted or exacerbated concerns in other areas. For example, frontline clerical and administrative staff, such as library assistants, are members of the large Public Services division, while subject librarians are members of Client Services. A split between professionally qualified and non-qualified staff is a potential area of concern in libraries, generally, as such a divide can lead to lack of clarity about lines of responsibility and, if un-addressed, undermine the homogeneity and seamless nature of service provision. Finally, there are some areas within Information Services that never organizationally converged, and others (such as the library enquiry desk and the IT help desk) that have subsequently de-converged. A review will show whether these issues can best be addressed and resolved by further restructuring, by fine-tuning the existing structure, by creating new policies and procedures, or by simple re-labelling and clarification.

The future of convergence at Bristol

Without a formal review, it is difficult to predict future changes to the structure and makeup of Information Services. As described above, there are issues and concerns that need to be addressed. There are also areas in which Information Services has undoubtedly been a success, enabling creative synergies and improved support for digital information. At the time of writing, the new Director of Information Services has recently been appointed to the more senior Deputy Registrar post in the University, in which her strategic remit includes not only Information Services, but also four additional academic and administrative support departments, making the need for a review more important. Nevertheless, it is more than probable that, for the foreseeable future, the existence of a joint strategic management team is here to stay.

Acknowledgement

This chapter is largely based on information provided by Geoffrey Ford who led the convergence process and was the first Director of Information Services. It also includes observations of the Information Services Senior Management Team, and was reviewed by Alison Allden, the current Director.

7

Flagship learning resources for the 21st century at the University of Hertfordshire

Di Martin

Over the past ten years the University of Hertfordshire has successfully implemented an ambitious learning resources strategy founded in the delivery of fully integrated computing, library and media academic support services within a cohesive physical and online learning environment, available 24 hours a day, seven days a week, on and off campus.

This strategy comprised four key interlinked strands:

- the exploitation and large scale use of computing technology for enhanced integrated services
- the creation of diverse attractive modern integrated study environments available 24/7
- extensive digital and print collections of information resources
- a new organizational structure to deliver integrated services and provide expert advice and support.

The achievement of this vision represented major change for the University, required senior level commitment and a central driving force focused on the appreciation of future student needs and expectations.

This case study describes the background to the strategy, our pioneering building and digital service developments and some of our experiences in achieving major change. The resulting impact on the University, its staff and students; on learning and teaching; and on subsequent developments are also outlined.

The University of Hertfordshire

The University of Hertfordshire is one of the UK's 'new' universities. It is a large multi-campus, multi-disciplinary organization with over 20,000 students and 1800 staff about 20 miles north of London. Undergraduate and post-graduate study programmes and research activities cover a wide range of subject disciplines. There is a diverse student population studying in a variety of full-time and part-time modes, at different levels and spanning a wide age range.

Circumstances leading to convergence and change

Growth in student numbers

Until the early 1990s the University was one of the smallest higher education institutions in the UK. At that time Government policy led to a massive expansion in student numbers in higher education in the UK. Nationally student numbers increased by some 70%, but at Hertfordshire the growth was much higher with student numbers rising from some 7000 to almost the present 20,000 over a four-year period. As a result the demand on library and computing services also grew dramatically and the existing provision rapidly proved inadequate. At national level, the serious impact of this massive increase in student numbers on academic library provision prompted the UK Higher Education Funding Councils to instigate a review of academic library provision. The resulting Follett report (Joint Funding Councils' Libraries Review Group, 1993) made a number of practical recommendations for academic library development and national funding was made available for a capital building programme and for a programme of research into IT development, known as the Electronic Libraries Programme (eLib). At Hertfordshire, drawing on the recommendations of the national report and the opportunity to bid for a funding contribution towards a proposed new building, we were determined to look ahead and to create the academic 'library' of the future to support the achievement of excellence in learning, teaching and research in the 21st century.

Estates strategy

As part of its expansion and subject diversification in this period, the University merged with a number of smaller institutions with varied computing, library and media arrangements. A new University Estates strategy led to the amalgamation of these colleges onto the University's existing campuses and the relocation of some existing departments. In particular, in 1995, the Law School moved to small new campus, in effect a 'greenfield site'. This opportunity prompted practical consideration of the computing, library and media services needed to support academic staff and students into the future in this new environment. A successful pilot implementation of a step change to fully integrated computing, library and media services with a new organizational structure at this small campus was valuable in informing the final planning of our wider full-scale implementation the following year.

A track record of successful co-operation

The success of this pilot implementation of fully integrated services owed much to the long track record of extensive co-operation at senior level between the existing separate computing and library services. There were mutual benefits in dealing jointly with the common issues arising from the delivery of centrally provided and funded institution-wide services. In addition, the University had had the foresight in the early 1990s to develop an institutional information systems strategy led by the Librarian, which resulted in a major computer network infrastructure implementation project that provided a practical vehicle for embedding co-operative working across the two services.

Student expectations

During this period a number of issues were emerging as imperatives for better co-ordination of service provision to students. Students were frustrated by having to move from library to computer centre depending on whether they were retrieving information or using computers to analyse, process and present that information, by the varied opening hours of the different existing services, and by the lack of co-ordinated support for online services. Furthermore, an analysis of enquiries made at the library enquiry desk and at the computing helpdesk revealed a substantial overlap and similar patterns in the questions being asked. In both cases some 70% of enquiries were routine, not requiring the specialist expertise of computing or information professionals.

As a result serious consideration was given to eliminating barriers to service accessibility and the definition of likely future student needs and expectations. Although we knew a great deal less then about use of the internet and the impact of the web, about electronic journals and digital information services and about virtual learning environments, nevertheless the signs for the future were clear. Over time these driving forces and their impact on changing student expectations have evolved to determine the continued development of our integrated service provision.

In today's 'google.com' 24-hour society, students expect value for money and immediacy, with quick and easy access to learning resources; in one place, whether physical or online; at times to suit them, day and night; and without queues, restrictions or other barriers. They also expect to integrate their social life with their study environment. Our learning resources provision has to meet these expectations.

Services included in the converged department
Our vision

In our vision of the future we decided we needed not only to bring together but to integrate fully all the central learning resources (computing, library and media) students needed for independent study to complement their formal teaching programmes. We wanted to meet student expectations of a seamless integrated environment for information gathering, information analysis, processing, recording, presentation and communication, available 24 hours a day, seven days a week, both on and off campus. We wanted to encourage study and academic achievement with attractive modern high capacity study environments that students would want to visit and spend time in. We also wanted to recognize the different study requirements and preferences inherent in a large diverse multidisciplinary community ranging from noisy groupwork activities to silent individual study.

Exploitation of the pervasive mass use of computing technology was central to the planning for our net-enhanced University. We wanted to use computing technology and digital resources not only to integrate services, but also to extend the study environment beyond the captivity of the four walls of our learning resources centres, both on and off campus. We wanted to provide integrated facilities and services 24 hours a day, seven days a week, and to deliver them as economically as possible in terms of staffing resources. We therefore adopted a self-service and self-help approach to the delivery of our core services and user support both to support 24/7 availability and off-campus use and to allow the use of our limited staffing resources to provide 'value-added', specialist services and support and to sustain partnership working with academic faculties.

The integrated services

The new department set up to realize this vision was called Learning and Information Services (LIS). The facilities and services managed by LIS that form the integrated services include:

- three learning resources centres (LRCs) with 2900 study places and some 1500 computer workstations
- integrated student desktop with single point access via personal login to a full range of networked online resources and services
- extensive digital and print library collections including 500,000 volumes of bookstock and 10,000 journal titles, most of which are available online
- computer network infrastructure and external communications across the University
- e-mail service
- central academic and administrative computer systems
- StudyNet, the University's managed learning environment (implemented in 2001)
- desktop computing support for University staff (added in 2000)
- media presentation facilities in teaching rooms across the University
- specialist media facilities including video studios, video conferencing, theatre and conference presentation support
- the Careers Advisory Service (added in 2003)
- copyright and licensing management.

Implementing the strategy

The initial achievement of this vision in 1996–7 meant massive change on three fronts all at the same time.

New services and technology

It was a challenge to design and deliver integrated services to the end-users that were readily accessible, easy to use and well supported. The following three examples illustrate approaches adopted for their practical implementation.

An integrated student desktop

We developed an integrated student desktop to provide a single point of access to all the University's online services from every study place with a computer workstation. On personal login, the integrated desktop provides access to the internet, e-mail, StudyNet (the University's online learning environment), a full range of common and specialist software applications, Voyager (the library system), e-journals, information databases, past exam papers, University information, printing, and so on. This development was essential to allow all resources to be used at all study desks and for students to be able to choose their study environment according to how they wished to study rather than according to the resources they needed to use.

An integrated helpdesk

The integrated helpdesk is designed to handle on demand all routine enquiries across the full range of LIS facilities and services. 'Visit the helpdesk' is Step 2 of three steps to help; Step 1 is 'Help yourself' and Step 3 'Ask a specialist'. The helpdesk staff are trained locally as multi-skilled experts in our facilities and services; they are not computing, information and media professionals. For service consistency the helpdesk is staffed by the core team for seven days a week, with some working Tuesday–Saturday and Sunday–Thursday contracts.

Self-help guides and self-service facilities

The encouragement of a culture of self-service and self-help was essential to sustain 24/7 service delivery and economy of staffing resources. Self-help guides cover as many core services and basic transactions as possible and as many core services as possible are available on a self-service basis without staffed alternatives, including lending services for book issue and return.

Relocation to new building

From the outset it was recognized that for the new integrated services to be successful they need to be delivered on campus from a single location. Given the growth in student numbers we also needed a significant increase in the number of study places with and without computing facilities organized to create the variety of study environments envisaged.

A large new prestigious learning resources centre (LRC) was opened on the Hatfield College Lane Campus in 1997 to meet both of these requirements. This provides 1600 study places, of which half (800) are equipped with computer workstations, all configured with the integrated student desktop. They are arranged in a variety of different study environments to provide for groupwork and noisy activities and a café study area through to silent individual study. Wireless networks throughout the building also support the use of personal laptops for access to the University's online services. On other campuses, existing buildings were altered and refurbished to achieve similar smaller LRCs. More recently a second new large prestigious LRC opened in 2003 at the University's new Hatfield de Havilland Campus.

Organizational re-structuring

It was clear from the degree of change proposed for our services that something more fundamental than a management merger or co-location of existing departments and staffs was required. The two previous separate departments of Computer Centre and Library and Media Services were also significantly different in structure, size and culture. The Library and Media Services department was the result of a previous management level merger but with service delivery continuing through separate units.

We decided to focus on a totally new department with a new organizational structure designed to deliver integrated services down to the frontline and to maximize the use of expert staff time for value added services and activities requiring specialist skills. In the new organizational structure we built in staffing arrangements, which included regular evening and weekend working, some Tuesday–Saturday and Sunday–Thursday jobs to support a consistent quality of service over seven days a week, particularly for the integrated helpdesk, and a regular management rota for evenings and weekend days to support staff delivering frontline services. We also built in some progression routes through the use of linked grade posts.

The re-structuring process

The preparation for the organizational changeover was consultative and extensive, but also difficult. Staff were invited to participate in determining future service provision and in the planning of the new building and facilities. Working groups looked at various aspects of planning for the facilities in the new building such as drawing up specifications for the helpdesk and evaluating study furniture. They visited other libraries and new buildings to help with this, but the tight timescales for the building work meant this had to be a rapid process.

Two consultation papers formed the basis for discussions with staff prior to arriving at the final arrangements for the proposed new organizational structure and the process for its implementation. The first paper was about future service provision and the second, drawing on the conclusions from discussion of the first, set out a draft organizational structure for delivery of the new services. Open meetings were held with staff to discuss the papers and to gather feedback. Overlapping with these discussions, training programmes in core IT skills were implemented for all staff to try and ensure there was a minimum, common foundation level of practical IT skills both to support future service delivery and to provide staff with the confidence and opportunity to seek appointment to jobs in the new organizational structure. LIS staff did recognize the need for change and espoused aspects of the future service vision, but their involvement in its planning and overt commitment to its achievement was diluted by concerns about the personal implications for themselves individually.

The final version of the new organizational structure was developed and costed by the University Librarian and the Director of the Computer Centre, working with a pro-vice-chancellor and the Director of Personnel. The process for its implementation was based on the complete cessation of all existing jobs in the two departments with staff applying in a competitive environment for a new job in the new LIS department. The new structure was totally different from the old and offered sufficient promotional opportunities for it to be impossible to slot staff automatically into roles in the new department. As many staff had no recent experience of writing a job application or of a job interview, training days were arranged to assist staff in this process and over 95% of the staff took up this training opportunity. In the event over 60% of the staff were appointed to either a promotional post or a post with a further progression route. Where this was not the case, personal grades and salaries were protected; there were no redundancies. The re-structuring arrangements were negotiated and agreed with the recognized trades unions.

Staff reactions

LIS staff reactions were varied ranging from apparent denial that the change was taking place and the reinforcement of old job and territorial boundaries, through to excitement and impatience to get on with the new. Some staff pressed for more time to discuss future requirements and conversely others wanted the process speeded up to be able to 'just get on with it'. Some staff were confident and proud of their skills until the first days in their new jobs, when they suddenly felt vulnerable and thought they had had no relevant training or skills for the job. Some Computer Centre staff saw themselves as 'taken over' by the larger Library department, whereas some Library staff saw themselves 'taken over' by IT. Staff uncertainty, fear of change, lack of confidence, and the effect of losing the familiar was variously expressed and often in criticism of others. Those who were pleased with their appointments and promotions tended to remain quiet, so staff morale was not necessarily boosted by these positive outcomes. However, despite many predictions to the contrary, staff turnover during this time and subsequently was lower than in previous years and the new organizational structure has proved successful, not requiring any substantial amendment and allowing the flexibility to accommodate continuing development.

The senior staff of the two previous departments were perhaps in the most difficult position of all. They were themselves subject to the same change and the same implementation process as all the other staff, but at the same time had to implement the change, interview and appoint staff to jobs and positively progress all the developments. They were also carrying extremely high workloads to maintain service continuity, to achieve our technological developments and new services, to see through the fitting out and move to the new building as well as implementing a new organizational structure.

Some observations on the resulting impact of our changes
Scale and pace of change

There is no doubt that we achieved what we set out to do, but it is worth asking whether we were over-ambitious in trying to do too much at once and what effect that may have had on the change process itself. The sheer amount of change probably did become a barrier to the change process in two ways. First, the several different strands of change – new building, new services and technology, new organizational structure – allowed staff to focus more on one of these areas at the expense of the others. The scale of the new building project alone demanded a great deal of time and attention but it was easier to deal with than the human resource issues of the organizational re-structuring. Those staff who might have been excellent facilitators and champions of the new organizational structure were often too busy with other aspects of the change. Second, despite a clear focus on the importance of communications, the scale and pace of all the changes together did impact on LIS staff. They variously felt it was difficult to keep abreast of what was happening or overwhelmed by information. It was also hard to keep our customers up to date with what was happening in a meaningful way. However, even with this hindsight, it is hard to conceive how such a major and necessary step change could have been successfully achieved in any other way.

Students

The impressive scale and stunning design of the LRC building provided a new focus on the campus and makes a clear statement about the excellence of the University's learning resources. The building and integrated services have proved very popular with students. The University's student feedback questionnaire about central services records the highest satisfaction scores for learning resources provision. The high use of the LRC buildings, which has continued despite the parallel exponential increase in off-campus and online service use, also confirms that it is fulfilling expectations.

The ever-changing population of students, however, offers us a salutary lesson. They do not compare the LRCs and our integrated services with the University's previous provision and recognize a massive step change. Their expectations are based on seeing current provision as the normal standard and then wanting more. This drives home to us the constant need to review, enhance and change in the light of student feedback. The forward vision and built-in flexibility of our arrangements has proved dependable in supporting ongoing development and change.

Academic staff

Initially it was considerably harder to get academic staff to exploit the potential of the enhanced and integrated learning resources provision. The pace of change had been rapid and, with hindsight, we probably did not do enough initially to ensure that academic staff understood and embraced the changes we were implementing. There was also understandably an element of envy of the University's investment going into central learning resources and not into their specific discipline area. LIS works closely in partnership with faculties and academic staff to identify and meet the expectations of staff and students across all subject disciplines. Academic staff are encouraged to work with their students in the LRC and the key liaison focus of some LIS staff roles enhance this structured forward planning and co-ordination of resources provision and development.

Teaching and learning

At the time of planning the building, it seemed there was no clear view of future teaching and learning requirements into the 21st century. However, since the LRC opened with its integrated learning resources provision, academic course teams have built the benefits into their teaching. In some cases coursework has changed to require students to take advantage of the integrated learning resources provision. The integrated student desktop has been extended to incorporate specialist software and online facilities available in faculty computing laboratories used for teaching, so that students can continue the work started in timetabled teaching sessions in the LRC at other times to suit themselves. From this further developments have emerged for co-ordination of software versions, universal printing accounts for students and computing standards across the University.

The major implementation of StudyNet, the University's managed learning environment, led by LIS, has further strengthened the integration of learning resources with the academic process with academic staff delivering online materials for student use in the LRC and at home. LIS staff work with academic staff to link information resources with course materials and teaching programmes within this online learning environment. The LIS integrated services and LRCs were a major stimulus for the development of the online learning environment and a University-wide approach to the achievement of an excellent holistic student learning experience.

University and its reputation

Without University senior management commitment and investment, the realization of this ambitious learning resources strategy and our LRC buildings would not have been possible. However, as with all businesses, the University was clearly looking for a substantial return on its investment. The new LIS services and LRC buildings have delivered that substantial return in several ways:

- The new LRC provides a central focus on campus and an impressive flagship building highly regarded by staff and students.
- The physical building and the integrated services have the flexibility to support and respond to change.
- The services and buildings are a major external PR focus receiving interest and visitors from all over the world.
- They have played a central role in promoting the further development of teaching and learning.
- They have contributed to the achievement of maximum external quality assessment scores for the University for learning resources.
- Perhaps most importantly, these changes have greatly enhanced the students' learning experience and gained their very positive customer satisfaction.

Lastly, it is important to note that without the strong commitment, hard work and expertise of the LIS staff we would not have achieved these massive changes nor the continuing digital service developments, which have followed so successfully since.

References

Bunn, R. (1998) Intellect Inside: University of Hertfordshire LRC building analysis, *Building Services Journal*, January, 22–5.

Joint Funding Councils' Libraries Review Group (1993) *Report* (the Follett Report), Bristol, HEFCE.

Martin, D. (2003) Supporting Independent Learning: the pioneering new design at the University of Hertfordshire. In *Libraries as Places: buildings for the 21st century. Proceedings of the thirteenth seminar of IFLA's Library Buildings and Equipment Section together with IFLA's Public Libraries Section. Paris, France 28 July–1 August 2003*, 73–88.

Spring, M. (1997) One Day All Libraries Will Be Like This, *Building*, 21 November, 40–4.

8

Convergence at King's College London

Margaret Haines, Patricia Methven, Jean Yeoh

Introduction

The College

King's College London is one of the two oldest and largest colleges of the University of London: a major multi-faculty university institution with some 19,200 students and 5000 staff, it has a leading position in UK higher education and a worldwide reputation for research and teaching.

The College has grown and developed through mergers with several institutions, each with its own distinguished history. These include: the United Medical and Dental Schools of Guy's and St Thomas' Hospitals (UMDS); Chelsea College; Queen Elizabeth College; and the Institute of Psychiatry. There are currently ten schools at King's. Six are health science schools; the others are: Humanities, Law, Physical Sciences and Engineering, and Social Science and Public Policy.

Information Services and Systems

Information Services and Systems (ISS) reports to the College Secretary and Registrar and is part of a larger Academic Services Directorate, which includes the King's Institute for Learning and Teaching (KILT) as well as the Academic Registry. ISS incorporates three teams led by Deputy Directors (of Information Systems, Customer Services, and Archives and Information Management) and a Corporate Services team, which is line-managed by the Director.

It is important to note that, while ISS has responsibility for web services, corporate records and legal compliance, it does not have responsibility for many of the other academic services, which are often included in converged services. For example, ISS is not responsible for Management Information Systems (which reports to the Director of Resources); desktop support (which is provided by each school); AV/media; telecommunications; or room bookings.

ISS produces three-year strategic and business plans alongside a yearly operational plan, and also leads the development and implementation of the College's Information and Knowledge Strategy. ISS has just produced its three-year Strategic Plan for 2004–7 and is about to consult on the Information and Knowledge Strategy for 2005–10. One recommendation of the latter is to integrate ISS with some of the other information functions, such as Management Information Systems (MIS).

History of convergence
Early structures

The current structure of ISS fits well into a totally converged model, but the structure has evolved over many College mergers and restructuring processes. Before 1984, the computing and library services were separately managed. In 1985, the merger of Queen Elizabeth College and Chelsea College with King's resulted in the merger of the three libraries into a single structure and the three computing departments into a single Computing and IT Services (C&IT) department. Derek Law was appointed in 1984 as University Librarian to oversee the merger and then to manage the converged library service, which also included the King's College London Archives. The Archives team had dual reporting lines: through the University Librarian to the Principal for the Liddell Hart Centre for Military Archives, and direct to the College Secretary and Registrar for matters relating to the College's own archives. Meanwhile, Andrew Byerley was appointed Director of C&IT. Library Services reported to the Principal of the College, while C&IT reported to the College Secretary and Registrar.

In 1984 the free-standing King's College Hospital Medical School was reunified with King's College London. King's College Library Services continued to serve the Hospital, and King's College Archives contracted with the Hospital Trust to manage their historical records. This is the situation today.

In 1992, various factors caused the College to consider converging the library and computing services. This was the period of the first Follett report, and there was a general consensus that the information future lay in the interface of a powerful library – IT environment and that Follett would be likely to recommend converged services. When Arthur Lucas took over as College Principal, he decided to create a Department of Information Services and Systems. In 1993, Derek Law took on the new role of Director of Information Services and

Systems, reporting directly to the Principal. The Director of ISS met regularly with the Directors of Library Services and C&IT to enable more concrete planning for integration across ISS. The College set up a review group to advise on the appropriate structure for ISS and on the services it should provide and support. This led to more formal integration of the electronic information services provided by Library Services and C&IT, and an Electronic Information Projects Group was established at the start of the 1994–5 session. The College also set up an ISS Strategy Committee in 1994, led by Professor Barry Ife (Vice-Principal, later Acting Principal in 2003–4), but continued separate Library and Computing Services committees until 1999.

In 1997 the Institute of Psychiatry joined King's and in 1998 the College merged with the United Medical and Dental Schools of Guy's and St Thomas' (UMDS). Another ISS structure was created from the merger of the two library and computing services, and it was recognized that some academic services would need to be extended to the Institute of Psychiatry, for example network and archives support.

In the model of ISS that resulted from this merger, there were three main teams (Computing, Library and Archives) reporting to the Director of Information Services and Systems. This cleaned up the reporting lines and allowed for better articulation of how the Archives team could support the College's information governance needs in the light of new legislation – through the delivery of adequately funded archives, records management and legal compliance services. Convergence was taken one step further in this model, with the school-focused service teams reporting to *both* the Director of C&IT *and* the Director of Library Services. However, as reported by one of the senior managers, this new level of convergence was not without its challenges. One such challenge was the increasing involvement of staff in each other's areas of work, something that generated a degree of tension until issues of demarcation and duplication of work were resolved. Other issues that were addressed during this restructuring period included the need to provide a consistently high quality of service at all times, including weekends, even in the absence of the relevant staff, and the need to co-ordinate IT training not only across library and computing services but across the entire College (Milne, 1998).

Derek Law left King's in 1998 and a new Director, Alan MacDougall, was appointed in 1999, reporting to the College Secretary and Registrar rather than to the Principal.

The 2001 restructuring proposals

In 2000, Alan MacDougall commissioned a strategy review of ISS from Emmerson Consulting Limited. The key findings of this review were that:

- Schools in the College did not regard ISS as a cohesive organization about which they had a single unified view. Rather they saw it as an umbrella for three discrete services about which they held very different views.
- The recently established focused services were seen as a success and the schools were keen to see these extended and developed.
- In order to meet customer expectations, to win the hearts and minds of customers and stakeholders, and to be provided with a larger share of College resources, ISS needed to undertake a radical rethink of its aims, objectives, organization, attitudes and approaches.

This review identified strategic objectives and critical success factors for ISS, which were later incorporated into the ISS Strategic Plan 2001–4, launched in April 2001. The Plan was developed in the context of the College's own Strategic Plan, the College's Information Strategy and widespread consultation with users. Its aim was to focus ISS resources on delivering core services well and on achieving better customer support. The new mission for ISS was 'supporting excellence in the College's information infrastructure'.

The ISS Strategic Plan identified the resources required to deliver the plan, and clarified within this what was required for mission critical services. Unfortunately, the College was not able to find the level of resources required for the complete vision, and the ISS Directorate Board therefore prepared a proposal for implementation of the Strategic Plan, which reflected the financial constraints. Just one of the implications of this was the elimination of ISS-managed desktop support to the schools (desktop support is now provided by the schools themselves). The proposal was presented to staff in July 2001 and marked the beginning of a long period of consultation with staff and unions over the new structure, ending in late 2001.

The structure that was developed to implement this plan moved ISS towards greater convergence in several ways, for example by integrating the IT and Library helpdesk services, by partially converging information specialist support to the schools and by creating a Corporate Services team to deliver personnel and finance support across all of ISS.

The plan was implemented in 2001–2 and, as with previous organizational changes, was not without its challenges. These included: protracted negotiations with the unions about the loss of posts; the downgrading of some posts; and arrangements for voluntary severance for those made redundant. When new technical posts could not be filled internally, ISS faced the additional challenge of recruiting staff in the context of a very competitive market in London. As late as 2004, some of these posts were still filled with contract staff. The last remaining staff member to take voluntary redundancy did so in the late spring of 2004.

After the 2001 restructuring

The Director of ISS responsible for the convergence plan in 2001, Alan MacDougall, left King's in December 2002. The Director of the Information Resources and Services (IRS) team, Anne Bell, became acting Director of ISS for five months until she left King's in the Spring of 2003. At this point, the Director of Archives and Corporate Records Services (ACRS), Patricia Methven, was asked to manage IRS, and the Director of Information Systems, David Clyde, became acting Director of ISS until September 2003 when a new Director, Margaret Haines, was appointed.

During this time, two senior posts in the IRS team also became vacant and there were ongoing gaps among the Information Systems and ACRS team leaders. The net result of all these vacancies was a serious gap in the senior management team. Fortunately, in late 2001–2, a consultant was hired to help with the restructuring process and to ensure that ISS fully developed its business and strategic planning processes. This consultant, Bryan Harrison, provided much needed continuity and direction for the senior team and also provided support to the new middle management team across ISS.

It would have to be said that the senior-level gaps did cause a significant loss of momentum immediately after restructuring (dispiriting for staff who were enthusiastic about moving forward) and helped to foster lingering resentment among those staff who were unhappy about the changes. The remaining members of the senior management team had to make some hard decisions based around a more limited range of priorities. Nonetheless there were some significant developments during that time, such as the introduction of a rigorous business planning process, the rolling out of personal development plans across ISS to focus staff on career and skills development, a series of team away days which also supported the team-building effort and the establishment of many cross-ISS groups for operational and strategic planning.

Opportunities for voluntary redundancies also allowed for the recruitment of new staff who brought different experiences and knowledge to the team.

Fine-tuning the model in 2004

When Margaret Haines arrived in September 2003 many senior posts were still vacant. This presented her with an opportunity to examine the overall impact of the restructuring and to make any necessary adjustments. In the autumn of 2003, the new Director met all ISS teams and interviewed every head of school and administrative department in the College to determine their views of ISS and, in particular, their views about the restructuring. The main findings from outside ISS were that there was still no clear understanding within the College of the role of the School Support Services team, that there were concerns that ISS was not fully responsive to user needs and that there was some misunderstanding about how ISS spent its budget, particularly on IT infrastructure.

Internal comments from ISS staff indicated that communication across ISS was felt to be poor, and that there were still some teams for whom changes in structure were problematic because of issues of size.

The new Director proposed three immediate changes to the structure:

- that the Corporate Services team should report directly to her, enabling her to review and reprioritize the budget and have a direct input into staff development – including the proposals for personal development plans and performance management plans
- that responsibilities across the senior management team needed to be more balanced
- that there needed to be a very explicit and clearly visible commitment to customer services, including explicit support to research and e-learning.

This resulted in a revised model, which introduced a Customer Services team made up of the Site Services team and a restructured School Support Services team. The latter was divided into three teams re-named Research and Learning Development, Research and Learning Liaison, and Training and Enquiry Support Services. The first of these teams provides dedicated research and e-learning support across the College. Meanwhile, the Information Resources team was moved to form part of the Archives and Information Management team, alongside ACRS.

The current model

In choosing a model of convergence to describe ISS today, ISS is closest to Terry Hanson's Model 2 – it is converged at deputy director level, but the Deputy Directors do have considerable autonomy within a common strategic framework.

ISS is working towards Model 3, where service is integrated throughout the department. Traditional library and IT helpdesks have merged but require cross-team support to provide an adequate level of service. The best way of achieving this cross-team support without having a negative effect on other services is being considered. Many cross-ISS working groups have been established to bring those staff working in common areas together: for example, there are groups for e-learning; collection development; staff development; quality standards and service improvement; legal compliance; and business continuity. These groups draw together staff from all levels within ISS, and efforts are being made to ensure commitment from all parts of the department.

During the next five years, organizational effort in ISS will be directed towards the development of common departmental values, and towards an understanding of the role that the department should play both in the institution and in the wider information community. Without this commitment to common professional values, ISS is unlikely to achieve Hanson's Model 3.

Conclusions

Lessons learnt

Over the last 20 years, ISS has experienced many organizational changes, which have gradually moved it towards the converged service we know today. It is difficult to comment on lessons learnt from these changes when they are not personal experiences – only one of the three authors of this case study has worked in all of the different permutations of the ISS organizational model. Consequently, many of the lessons learnt come from ISS folklore.

It is important to note that some of the lessons listed below were anticipated at the outset, for example the importance of consultation with the unions and of ensuring that other departments and schools were kept informed. Inevitably, not all staff were comfortable with the changes that restructuring brought, although most did agree with the general direction of travel.

Some of the common themes which have emerged from the different organizational changes over the last few years are as follows:

• Staff need to feel supported during periods of change, especially in terms of airing and dealing with negative feelings.
• The unions have a significant role to play both in terms of supporting the changes and in terms of assisting staff left without jobs to find new roles.
• There is a need to take time out to make each different stage of restructuring work before embarking on the next.
• There is a need for constant reinforcement of the reasons for the change for some time after restructuring has taken place.
• Outside, impartial advice for both middle and senior managers has an important part to play throughout the process in keeping them on track with planning, and in providing an important safety valve for taking some of the stress off of those involved.
• There is a need to help staff recognize different professional cultures and to find ways to identify common values.

- It is important to devote time and resources to getting key messages across in an open style, which suits all levels of staff, using a variety of delivery methods, for example e-mails, staff meetings and inviting written questions.
- Staff need to be reassured that periods of apparent inactivity are often due to unavoidable delays, sometimes caused by personnel procedures, and do not mean that further bad news is looming.
- There is a need to ensure that schools and departments are aware of what is being planned and are briefed at every stage so that they are clear about the benefits of convergence, especially in terms of student learning and research support.

Benefits

Despite the angst inevitably associated with the restructuring, the move to convergence has brought undeniable benefits. These have not yet been formally evaluated – a project in itself to be undertaken during the next strategic planning phase. However, ISS management feels that the move to a converged structure has facilitated better strategic planning across the various functions and has allowed for full ISS participation in planning for e-learning, business continuity and legal compliance issues. It has also improved the management of ISS staff and financial resources, and has afforded an opportunity to review and address other aspects of ISS including an evaluation of staff development work through an Investors in People assessment, a major user survey, a review of health and safety practices across ISS and a review of financial processes in our information services centres.

All of this has helped demonstrate to the schools and to the rest of the College that ISS is serious about evaluation, about listening to users, and about transparency and providing value for money. This has not only increased ISS's credibility in the College but has also raised its profile.

Other benefits of convergence included:

- a broadening of the skills base for those staff providing the enquiry service, and potentially for information specialists engaged in research and e-learning support
- clearer management lines and accountability across ISS
- greater involvement in management processes for middle and senior managers, and opportunities to share good management practice
- more understanding and respect across ISS for the challenges faced by other teams and for the work that they do
- a joint approach to staff development across ISS and therefore more equitable access to development opportunities

- better discussion of the 'invisible' services, such as network services, because these are now part of a more visible overall converged package of information and knowledge services
- greater appreciation for the role that ISS fulfils in supporting King's as an organization, for example ISS's contribution to business continuity and legal compliance, disability developments, web marketing and knowledge management
- the leadership role and centrality of ISS in major College strategic developments
- clear emergence of a now dominant sentiment that the converged service has common goals that are user driven
- deepened understanding that a successful communication strategy for users involves a great deal more than putting information on the web and circulating papers
- identification of areas where the scope for cross-fertilization within ISS is particularly rich, such as the web, content management, information security and the training of non-ISS staff.

Final thoughts

King's College London has a long history of mergers. One of the consequences of this has been that ISS has been engaged in a constant process of restructuring for the last 20 years. Every phase of that restructuring has moved the department one step closer to true convergence of a range of information services (IT, library, archives and records management to name but a few) although some information services still remain outside the ISS portfolio.

In the broader context, convergence has brought important benefits to the College. A converged ISS is better able to support College visibility in a global marketplace and enhance competitive advantage to help meet increased student expectations of 24/7 access to e-learning environments. Convergence has supported improvements to College information governance and the exploitation of College knowledge assets and research. We expect that these benefits will increase as we move towards greater convergence.

We believe that true convergence requires an acceptance of common professional values, including evidence-based and reflective practice. The next ISS Strategic Plan will emphasize the pursuit of common values and service ethics and the added value of convergence to the College. Key steps to be taken include:

- the creation of a cohesive management team, including both middle and senior management

- the development of a common set of skills for those information staff in front line roles
- the creation of a communications strategy so that there is a more proactive but consistent approach to representing ISS inside and outside King's
- the production of protocols for working across teams on common tasks such as e-learning and collection development
- the creation of a programme to ensure a deep understanding across all ISS staff of the contribution that they can and do make to the goals of the College.

Reference

Milne, R. (1998) New Media and IT Developments: managing the change, *Bibliothek Forschung und Praxis*, **22** (3), 341–5.

Acknowledgements

The authors would like to thank Anne Andrews, Executive Assistant to the Director of ISS, for her assistance with the editing of this chapter. They would also like to thank David Clyde, Derek Law, Alan MacDougall, Harry Musselwhite and Anne Bell for reviewing the chapter.

9

Converging to support learning at Newport

Janet Peters

Brief description of institution

With its origins as a mechanics institute, the University of Wales Newport, can trace its birth to 1841. The institute was succeeded by a technical college, which joined a teacher training college and an arts college in 1974 to form Gwent College of Higher Education. Degree awarding powers were obtained in 1996, together with a change of name to University of Wales College, Newport. Since May 2004 the new name is University of Wales Newport, reflecting our new status as a full member of the federal University of Wales.

Located on two main campuses, one in Newport and the other on its outskirts at Caerleon, the University teaches in all subject areas except medicine. Recently, a branch of the Community University of the Valleys (East) has been established in Tredegar, through which many of the University's outreach programmes are operated, enabling the achievement of our mission 'to bring learning to the heart of our communities'. Approximately a third of the University's 9500 students are based in further education colleges throughout Wales and overseas.

Newport is unusual in its high proportion of part-time students (over 50%) and in the overall age profile, with only 10% under 20 and 50% over 30 years of age. The largest subject areas are in art, media and design, teacher education (particularly primary) and business studies.

Predominantly a teaching-led university, Newport's School of Art, Media and Design obtained a Grade 5 in the last Research Assessment Exercise, the highest grade awarded in the UK. Other research areas are archaeology and mechatronics, although research activity is now being encouraged by all schools, particularly in applied areas.

Circumstances leading to convergence

Prior to convergence, there had been various permutations of the services involved. On my appointment in 1990, the Library was a separate service; there was no central IT provision; and there was a small media resources unit linked to the teacher training area. In 1994 the media resources unit joined the Library on the retirement of its head, and the post was not replaced. From 1995 an IT centre was established, as part of the implementation of the Information Strategy, which recognized the need for a centralized computer network, which would serve both the academic and the administrative needs of the College. The head of the centre was, unusually, managed by an information strategy steering group of very senior staff, who oversaw and funded the creation from scratch of a modern IT network. Staff, who had been deployed in academic faculties to support local IT facilities, were transferred to join the new centre, and several new appointments were made.

In 1998 the University decided to establish a centre for learning development (CLD), and to locate it within the Library, which was perceived to be a neutral, subject independent base, with an existing ethos of supporting learning. The new service became Library and Learning Resources. At the same time, the media resources unit was transferred to the IT centre to form the new IT and Media Service. Library and Learning Resources staff reported initially to the Principal and then to the Deputy Principal, while IT and Media Service staff reported to the Assistant Principal (Corporate Services).

The notion of the current converged department was proposed in 2001 during a period when the University was implementing a recovery plan. The Head of Library and Learning Resources was given the task of working with the Head of IT and Media Services to achieve the following aim: 'IT and Media Services to be merged with Library and Learning Resources, restructured, and consideration to be given to a greater focus on student learning infrastructure' (UWCN, 2001, 15).

The Head of IT and Media Service was to report to the Head of Library and Learning Resources with immediate effect. Full merger and change of focus were to be achieved by March 2002.

The purpose of the merger was to create a new streamlined approach to the support of learning in a variety of ways, especially given that the boundaries between information in libraries and on computers were becoming blurred. The University was in the process of implementing a virtual learning environment (VLE), and it was felt that this needed a co-ordinated approach by all of the academic services if it was to be successful. It had also been noted that the dual reporting lines did not aid a unified approach. For example, opening hours were inconsistent between the services, publicity was very different, and students were often not informed of alternative provision in the 'other' service where it might have been appropriate. At the same time, with the arrival of a new Vice-Chancellor, there was also a trend for a smaller number of larger departments within the University as a whole.

There was certainly no money for additional staffing, nor for an expensive restructuring, but the direct saving of money was not a short-term objective. The major cost saving lay in the opportunity cost for the Assistant Principal, who no longer had to spend time on overseeing the IT and Media Service. It was also assumed (although without any concrete evidence) that some duplication of effort could be avoided.

The decision was discussed by the Principal at the time with the heads of the services prior to being implemented, and would not have happened without the agreement of both. However, the Head of IT and Media Service only accepted the apparent demotion because of working part time. It was not an easy decision to make, although the personal working relationship between the heads remained positive at all times. If agreement had not been reached, the post would probably have been advertised.

Both heads requested advice from the members of SCONUL and UCISA, together with similar groups in Wales, on the benefits and pitfalls of convergence. The response was mixed in terms of the advantages, with most replies emphasizing the influence of local circumstances. Horror stories of major restructurings being attempted very quickly and alienating staff were encountered in a few cases. We considered ourselves fortunate in that we had been given a year to plan, and that solutions were not being imposed on us from above. Many colleagues sent us staffing charts, and explanations of what had worked and what had not, which were invaluable.

External advice was also obtained from Hirshon (1998), a reference obtained from a staff development programme on 'Managing for strategic change' attended by the Head of Library and Learning Resources in 1999. Various publications were also referred to (Edwards, Day and Walton, 1998; Law, 1998; Williams, 1998), which indicated success factors and explained how convergence could improve services if implemented effectively.

We obtained feedback from University staff by circulating a consultation paper to find out what they would like to see from a joint service. The main suggestion was that there should be more support for electronic learning, both for staff and students. There were also comments that both services were working well, so any changes should be introduced gradually to avoid disruption. This was particularly important in the light of our student profile, which at the time was not confident in the use of IT. Interestingly, senior managers seemed to be more enthusiastic about major restructuring (although no budget was available to support this). We also asked a selection of students how library services and IT services could be improved, and again they were positive about the existing services. They asked for longer opening hours; more technical support; more library training; more guides; simpler logging on; more books, journals and PCs; and a refreshment area.

We also wanted to try to take our staff along with us in deciding how to operate with a 'greater focus on student learning'. We established a project group and organized visits to three broadly similar-sized universities. One had been fully converged for some time, one was managerially converged only and one had converged more recently. These visits were invaluable; details of what we learned and how this influenced the change process are included under 'Other observations' on page 83.

The planning process was reported to the Information Strategy Working Group, but by and large the two managers were allowed to develop proposals independently. Issues that arose from time to time were discussed with the Deputy Vice-Chancellor, who was tasked with implementing the actions in the recovery plan.

Services included

Newport includes a wide range of services within the department of Library and Information Services, spread across two campuses. These are Library Services, IT and Media Services (including administrative computing), the Centre for Learning Development, the Distance Learning Centre and the Print and Copy Services.

The model adopted

Library and Information Services (LIS) at Newport report to a Director of LIS, who sits on the University's management board and who is executively responsible for all aspects of the service. The post used to report to the Deputy Vice-Chancellor, but now reports to the Pro-Vice-Chancellor (Academic), who is also the line manager for the deans of schools. This has the advantage of creating links between the academic and learning support functions, which is proving to be useful.

Within LIS the structure is divided into three, each with its own manager. Library Services, IT and Media Services and the Centre for Learning Development have a large degree of autonomy, including separately allocated budgets, but discuss strategy and ethos within the LIS Management Team (consisting of the Director of LIS and the three heads). The Director of LIS also holds regular meetings with each head to discuss and agree operational issues. Each service operates on both University campuses, but, significantly, accommodation is not shared. This has seriously restricted the scope for joint working. Requests for building work to be done to provide a shared entrance area on one of the campuses have so far not been seen as a priority for development. This may change in the future if proposals for a new campus come to fruition.

Before adopting the current structure, various possible alternative structures were tested with staff, but in each case the small number of staff with particular skills made any reorganization potentially disruptive to the service. I certainly did not want to restructure just for the sake of it. However, we did need to improve the focus on learning, and also to provide a more streamlined service for students, so some small but significant changes were made. These included the creation of two new information assistant posts, which would provide frontline support in IT for students using the computer suites. Selected for their customer service skills, these staff would also free up the time of the technical staff, who could spend more time behind the scenes dealing with reported faults. The posts were created from two former ones, which had been frozen some time before. The other change was to establish department-wide working groups. Each of these had a cross-sectoral theme: staff development and training; marketing and publicity; electronic resources; disabilities support; student training; VLE development. Members were sought from all three services, and chairs appointed. With the exception of the VLE group, none of the groups was chaired by a member of IT and MS staff, despite extensive encouragement.

Some changes were also made to the senior staff roles: the former Head of Library and Learning Resources became the Director of Library and Information Services, the former Campus Librarian at the larger campus became the Head of Library Services, covering both campuses, and the Campus Librarian at the other campus took on the additional role of Quality Manager for LIS as a whole. The PC Support Supervisor was promoted to become PC Support Manager, adding the technicians looking after Macintosh machines to his responsibilities. One of the campus-based PC Team leaders became responsible for student computing services across both campuses and the other took on computing services for staff, again on both campuses.

Once the new structure was in place, a series of away days were organized where staff came together to brainstorm our strengths and weaknesses and to highlight our areas for development. These sessions have determined our strategy and annual action plans for the last two years.

Experience and lessons learned

The model has served us well for the initial two years, in that there has been no disruption to services and cross-departmental working has been established in the working groups. Evidence from the latest student satisfaction survey in 2002 indicated much higher levels of satisfaction with LIS than two years before (although this was probably due to new computer suites, which were installed prior to the convergence). The profile of Library and Information Services has been raised in the sense that it is now represented directly on the management board, the main executive body for the University. However, there have been problems, some of which are not yet resolved.

The process has tested various personal skills, including tact and diplomacy, patience and persistence, sometimes to the limit! However, the new structure has been thoroughly discussed in various forums and committees, as part of the extensive consultation process, and accepted within LIS in principle at least.

In practice, some of the IT staff feel that their work is less well recognized than before and that they have lost professional status. While library staff gain some kudos from working in a university, IT staff seem to want to be valued for their professional expertise, regardless of the environment in which they work. Even though the separate name and to a large extent the identity of the IT and Media Services department have been retained, there is a feeling that the staff have become less employable. The fact that none has left since the convergence may indeed prove the point (or indicate that perhaps there are compensations).

Another difficulty remains in overcoming the idea that staff are 'too busy' to participate in meetings, to forward plan, to describe and evaluate services for users and, particularly, to participate in staff development. I would like to move towards the provision of a more considered, well-documented service, which has realistic targets, rather than fighting fires. I would also like staff to be aware of good practice in the sector and to be more aware of the work of the University, which can only be achieved by staff development and regular updating. Implementing this has been difficult, but progress is being made slowly. The problem is particularly acute with IT based services, since everyone in the University is heavily dependent on a reliable network, e-mail and computer system, and so every problem appears to the customer to be a major one, making prioritization difficult. The heads of service do spend time on prioritizing work for their staff, which is essential, but it can mean that apparently less urgent jobs, which meet the needs of the wider service (such as, for example, producing user guides or updating the website), are not done in a timely fashion. The working groups have been successful in rectifying some of these issues, but unfortunately the majority of the work has actually been done by the library staff. It has been decided that the representation of IT staff on the working groups will be considerably increased in the coming year to try to improve this.

There have also been conflicts between developmental staff and those with more of a security maintenance role. This has been exemplified in the development of the VLE, which has required close collaboration between staff with differing roles and very different priorities. It did not help that the VLE software was not one of the main platforms in IT and Media Services (although it was shared with the e-mail system). It was therefore difficult to gain ownership of the VLE project from all of the staff necessary to develop it successfully. A group was established to air these issues and to establish ways of working, but it remained problematic. Without specialist technical knowledge, I found it difficult as a manager to help with this, and so had to hope that those involved could find suitable solutions. This was a new phenomenon for me because until then I had been able to pick up enough background knowledge about the issues to help with decision-making, and in deciding who was bluffing!

With the recent appointment of a new senior member of staff in IT and Media Services, who has experience of developing learning environments for another university, the decision has now been taken to use industry standard software for e-mail and to develop a managed learning environment (MLE) using Microsoft tools and existing expertise. A joint project team of technical and developmental staff has been established and is working well. Library staff are also involved since they are responsible for establishing the links to electronic resources from the MLE. The success of this group is partly down to the personalities involved, who are all committed to its success, but also to the more natural connections that are now being made between the elements of the converged service. The new student portal will provide a genuine connection between the services offered by LIS and the courses offered by the schools.

In many ways, the presence of the Centre for Learning Development within Library and Information Services constantly justifies the convergence by providing the glue that holds the other services together. By focusing on the support of learning and the learner, it emphasizes our common purpose and provides a valuable bridge between the technical and the academic aspects of our services. There has certainly been no pressure from the University for the services to de-converge.

As the head of a converged service, I believe that the qualities required stem from enthusiasm for the end-product. Without a firm belief that services to learners can be improved by bringing the separate functions together, it would be easy to falter in the face of natural resistance to change. As a librarian, having some knowledge of IT (I was a systems librarian) generally helps, although care needs to be taken to recognize the limitations of one's knowledge. It is equally important not to allow one's own professional background to dominate. An ability to delegate is essential given the wide range of skills that staff possess. Managers need to be trusted to look after their areas, with the head encouraging discussion of common issues, communication and the co-ordination of activity by means of a joined-up strategy. Finally, having the patience to sustain a long-term vision, despite temporary difficulties, would be useful.

Other observations

Overall, I am not sure whether it has been most effective to adopt a softly-softly approach to changing the structure of the services. Alternatives have been actively considered, especially with the Head of IT and MS, but they have not been considered workable with the staffing levels we have. To have radically changed the structure would also have been inconsistent with the comments received throughout the consultation that there was not too much wrong with the current structure, so why change it? Despite the assistance we received on our visits to other universities, we could not think of an obvious and low-cost solution that would have transformed our work, and so I decided to adopt an evolutionary approach instead, beginning with the new LIS Management Team, the working groups, and some changes to roles where individuals were willing to accept them.

We learned from our visits to other universities that true hybrid posts in converged services were a rarity, and most staff were still known as librarians or technicians, despite having similar job titles (such as information assistant or information officer). Whether the notion of hybrid 'learning advisers' will develop further remains to be seen, but it is a concept that will be difficult to implement at Newport until we can share accommodation and provide common information points. In the interim, we are trying to ensure a consistent approach to students by providing staff development for all frontline staff to ensure that they are aware of the full range of LIS facilities.

One of the elements of the consultation process over the proposed convergence concerned the department's name. All University staff (and some students) were asked to choose between various suggested names. 'Library and Information Services' was the clear winner, and was therefore adopted, although, interestingly, within LIS it aroused strong feelings of 'us' and 'them', which had not surfaced too blatantly before (although there were always undercurrents that the whole process was a takeover by the library).

Once the name had been agreed, the new structure put in place and a new 'image' identified (including a joint website and a logo), we have worked hard on a new LIS strategy, on 'joined up' annual reports, and on our services to students and staff. We need to carry out a survey of our customers to find out if we are meeting their needs, particularly for the IT services, which is planned for next year. We have begun to establish some shared budgets (for instance for staff development and for publicity materials), which are making the overall administration of the service more effective.

We also decided (on the suggestion of some of the staff) to aim to obtain the Charter Mark standard, which would encourage a focus on customer care issues across the department, and which would provide an external benchmark that was not connected to libraries or IT services. Unfortunately this has had to be postponed since the University has since decided to work towards the Investors in People (IiP) standard, with Library and Information Services early in the queue for assessment, and we could not focus on both at the same time. We plan to pick up the work on Charter Mark again in the near future as a joint target, which is relevant to our service as a whole. Meanwhile, the work on preparing for IiP is usefully helping staff to understand their role in the University better, and is strengthening the connection between the LIS objectives and their individual targets within the appraisal process.

Has convergence made a difference? I believe so, although there is still a long way to go. The cultural differences of librarians and technical staff are a powerful influence in limiting the amount of change that can be achieved and I believe that the structure now needs to be re-visited if further improvement is to be made. Once again, consultations will take place, but I believe that as a department we now have a better understanding of our role within the University and should be able to accommodate change more readily than two years ago. Time will tell.

References

Edwards, C., Day, J. and Walton, G. (1998) eLib's IMPEL2 Project: organisational structures and responses to change in academic libraries, *New Review of Academic Librarianship*, 4, 53–70.

Hirshon, A. (1998) *Integrating Computing and Library Services: an administrative planning and implementation guide for information resources*, CAUSE Professional Paper Series, #18, Boulder, CO, CAUSE.

Law, D. (1998) Convergence of Academic Support Services. In Hanson, T. and Day, J. (eds), *Managing the Electronic Library: a practical guide for information professionals*, London, Bowker Saur.

University of Wales College, Newport (2001) *Recovery Plan 2000/1–2004/5*, Newport, UWCN (internal document).

Williams, R. (1998) Case Study: University of North London. In Hanson, T. and Day, J. (eds), *Managing the Electronic Library: a practical guide for information professionals*, London, Bowker Saur.

10

Converged information services at Roehampton University

Sue Clegg

Roehampton University

Roehampton University is a campus-based university in south west London, with four founding colleges (Digby Stuart, Froebel, Southlands and Whitelands), each of which has its own unique style and community spirit. It offers a very flexible modular structure with over 1500 different degree combinations and has an excellent reputation for teaching, combined with a growing research profile. There are around 8000 students at Roehampton, with planned growth to 9000 by 2008–9, principally in postgraduate and overseas students. There are five schools: Arts, Business and Social Sciences, Education, Human and Life Sciences and the new Graduate School.

Roehampton gained taught (1993) and research (1997) degree awarding powers and changed its title from Roehampton Institute London to University of Surrey Roehampton for a three-year period as a federal university, before finally emerging as Roehampton University in 2004.

Circumstances leading to convergence of Information Services

Roehampton decided to move to a converged Information Services Department in 1996, when a vacancy arose following the resignation of the then Head of Library and Media Services. There were a number of reasons for the decision, including:

- a need for strategic direction and leadership across the University in these areas

- recognition of a need for a voice in senior management (neither the Head of Library and Media Services nor the Head of Computing were on the senior management team)
- recognition that changes in technology and services might be better served by a single department working together than eight that competed for resources
- a need for a change of attitude in some areas where a 'can't do' culture prevailed.

While there was discussion about the potential advantages and disadvantages of convergence in some units (such as Library and Media Services), it was not widely debated across the University, and was essentially an executive decision driven by three members of the Rectorate (the senior University team at the time). These were the Senior Pro Rector (Deputy Rector and Resources Manager), Pro Rector (to be line manager of the new Information Services) and the Secretary and Registrar. These post holders have now all left Roehampton and that may become a significant factor in the future of Information Services, as they were individually and collectively champions for Information Services, understanding the need for a strategic approach and exercising key influences within Roehampton University over a seven-year period.

External advice, through visits and discussions, was sought from a number of universities about the value and purpose of a converged Information Services and what units might be included within it. The University of Surrey Director of Information Services was invited to meet key managers who were likely to be in the converged service and the senior team used feedback from these activities to help inform the decision to converge and which units would make up the new department, before advertising the post of Director of Information Services.

At the time that convergence was being considered the institution was also beginning to develop its information strategy, following the Joint Information Systems Committee (JISC) model. Although individuals in units that sub-sequently made up Information Services were involved in discussions about the information strategy it is not considered that this was one of the factors that led to convergence at Roehampton. Subsequent to the appointment of the Director of Information Services this emphasis changed and the appointed Director took a major lead in information strategy developments and it became a significant influence on the way in which the department and corporate priorities were shaped.

What is converged at Roehampton?

Library and Media Services, including Lecture Room Equipment Services, had been converged for a number of years and had latterly also incorporated open access PC suites. To these were added Computing and Network Services, Management Information Systems, Telephony, Television Roehampton, Software and Web Services, Careers and Reprographics.

Significant changes for each area while it has been within Information Services include:

- *Library/LRC*. The Library has taken on the leading liaison role for the whole department through the network of academic liaison officers by: replacing the traditional subject librarians; developing the electronic agenda, in its infancy at the time of convergence; developing a 'one stop shop' approach for students; and multi-skilling of assistants to work across all front line services.
- *Media Services*. Support for lecture room equipment has moved from Media Services into Customer Services and the focus for the Media Services unit has moved to a more technical and graphics support service for students and staff. This unit recently merged with Television Roehampton.
- *Computing and Network Services*. Formerly underfunded and lacking an effective future strategy, this team has benefited considerably from being in a converged department with a stronger voice and a new 'can do' attitude, enabled by an almost entirely new team. Recently renamed Computing and Communications services (see Telephony, below) it has had significant funding for upgrading the data and voice networks, for a major expansion of central servers and associated appropriate space management. Additionally, three years ago the University moved to a system of replacing all PCs every four years on a lease system and Information Services was asked by the schools to manage this. Other significant developments during this period have included cabling up virtually all halls of residence, expanding the open access PC suites, wireless networking and making the IT help desk a frontline customer service for students and staff. Many of the developments in this area have been brought to the fore through the work of the Information Strategy Committee discussions, where it became clear that unless the infrastructure was strong, other aspects of managing information would never be effective and that resources need to be invested in these areas.
- *Management Information Systems*. This team has moved from largely supporting three core legacy systems in Finance, Registry and Human resources/payroll to a much broader based service supporting and

influencing the development of any system that is likely to have University-wide applications (such as timetabling, estates and a virtual learning environment). During the last seven years the unit has also overseen the introduction of replacement systems for the three core functions, and has benefited from the converged strategic approach to resourcing. Recently it has merged with web and software teams to become a new Information Systems and Support Service.

- *Telephony*. This unit had two functions, one of technical installations management and the other of providing switchboard services and management of call charges. The University took the decision to move to Internet Protocol Telephony (IPT) as data and voice moved inexorably closer together and this unit moved under the network manager. However, in a truly converged approach, although the technical support comes through Network and Systems, the switchboard services are staffed as part of Customer Services through use of casual students and Information Services assistants, while the call charging is managed by the Information Services Finance team.

- *Television Roehampton (TVR)*. TVR has benefited from a new high profile location next to the Learning Resources Centre (LRC), and as part of Information Services opened up physical links with the LRC so that evening and weekend access to the edit suites became possible for the first time. Additional resourcing for equipment has also been made possible, and strategically TV services were included in the first Computing, Information Technology and Media strategy (1998).

- *Software and web services*. Increasing emphasis on both areas led to it being separated in 1999 into two units: Software & IT Coaching and Web Services, each with their own development plan and growing team managed under different sections. The development of one-to-one point of use IT coaching was a significant outcome of the information strategy work requested by academics in particular. Recently the units have been rejoined, together with Management Information Systems, into a new division of Information Systems and Support Services, reflecting the way in which technology and support needs are developing at Roehampton.

- *Careers*. The Students' Union employment service was brought under Careers as a key service provided by the University and the unit became known as Employment and Careers. Subsequently the University's HEACF funding also brought Volunteering into this service area as well. The University has a strong agenda for careers and employment as part of its corporate plan.

There is much evidence of internal career development for individuals across Information Services arising as a consequence of convergence, which the Information Services management has celebrated. Examples of this include: Information Services Assistants (ISAs) being able to gain skills on the front line IT help desk, which have enabled some to progress to become IT support officers; other ISAs have gained promotion into roles within the Employment and Careers Service; an IT co-ordinator has been able to progress to become technical administrator for the department and PA to the Directorate; and Languages Centre casual student employees have been able to get permanent employment as ISAs.

University strategies

Roehampton developed a corporate strategy six years ago, together with a series of integrated strategies, five of which are the responsibility of Information Services: Information strategy, Communications and Information Technology strategy, Employment and Careers strategy, Employability strategy and the Learning Resources strategy.

Model for convergence

Strategic co-ordination and direction is vested in the Director of Information Services, loosely line managed by a pro-rector or pro-vice-chancellor (PVC). The PVC's role has been to act as a sounding board and champion, rather than to take a directional role, and the PVC has had no direct involvement in the resource management of Information Services, since the Director of Information Services has been a key member of the Principal Budget Holders' Policy Group (PBH).

The expectation from the University senior team was for a real convergence and not just for a number of disparate units to be managed by a single person; as a consequence Information Services has been constantly evolving its structure towards this end. This has included mergers of service groups as demonstrated earlier, as well as ongoing reviews and changes in post title and job descriptions, with flexibility across the integrated service being a key feature.

Examples of post title changes include:

* Learning Resources Assistants becoming Information Services Assistants, with multi-skilling in a number of different service areas a requirement for career progression or grade improvements in order to create the flexibility to manage the range of services.

- Subject Librarians becoming Academic Liaison Officers and now acting as the principal two-way conduit for the whole of Information Services with the schools.
- Posts such as Head of Computing ceasing to exist, and the two senior departmental posts below the Director becoming Assistant Directors with no specific portfolio, to demonstrate a holistic approach to the Department.
- As service teams merged, establishing a number of key manager posts called Heads of Service. These are the Head of Learning & Liaison, Head of Computing & Communications, Head of Employment & Careers, Head of Information Systems & Support, Head of Media Services and the Head of Staff Development & Communications.
- A post of Customer Services Manager (formerly Site Librarian for one site) carrying responsibility for all customer facing services, wherever they are line managed, to provide consistency across the service response.

Experience and lessons learned

Change management process

The change management process at Roehampton has been an evolving and challenging one. Initially, because there had been no University-wide debate and consequently no 'ownership' leading to the creation of Information Services, there were a number of wrong assumptions and inherent barriers, which had to be overcome. These ranged from academic comments such as 'I thought Information Services was just a concept not a reality' to active hostility.

The first some of the individual units knew about their involvement in an Information Services convergence was when they saw the public advertisement for the post of Director of Information Services. Other units, because of the constantly changing organizational structures at Roehampton, had already had ten line managers in as many years and saw this as merely another one in a long series and their response was inevitably tinged with some cynicism about continuity of change management approaches! Other units such as Library and Media Services saw convergence as a positive way to improve IT support. The IT team did not want convergence and the only benefit that they saw was that they could get some of the Library posts and bookfund reallocated to the IT area. In short, it was a difficult and complex inherited situation!

The brief to the new Director was to create a new converged structure within six months and to achieve in the first instance three things:

- a turnaround in the IT Department from a 'won't do' culture to a 'can do' culture

- all units taking a student-centred, customer-focused approach, looking broadly across the University
- creating a Communications and Information Technology (C&IT) strategy.

On the first issue, a risk strategy was agreed with the University's senior team and following discussions with the C&IT team the worst case risk scenario nearly came to pass, with many of the then C&IT team departing within the first nine months. However, the University is now in a significantly different and much stronger position than it had previously been, with much less risk, both because of attitude and cultural changes and because of the holistic and strategic vision given to IT.

Learning points

The strongest learning points for Information Services have been that:

- *Attitude matters*. A consistent, positive, professional, 'can-do' approach inspires confidence in the ability to deliver and manage resources.
- *Integrity matters*. Some people will always believe that a large budget area is to some extent 'feathering its own nest' at the expense of others. From the outset the Directors sought to take a position of integrity in which it could be demonstrated against any audit or investigation that this was not the case and that the investment that was being made was for University-wide benefit and not against agreed priorities.
- *Communication matters*. In order to achieve consistency in services, communication, both to users and especially to the Information Services staff across teams, matters vitally. This has been particularly important for technologists to learn, and we are all still learning how to do this better.
- *Student centredness matters*. Putting the student at the heart of what we are trying to do is key in the Roehampton environment but is sometimes at odds with the way in which staff perceive issues.
- *Location matters*. It was a strategic University decision to place the Learning Resources Centre (LRC) at the heart of the campus and for Digby Stuart College to give up a prime teaching and residential building to the University for use as its LRC. The University and Information Services have then made this a high profile and welcoming building into which all aspects of the Departmental work can be seen in a 'one stop' approach to services.
- *Institutional involvement matters*. Proactive involvement within the corporate organization has been very important and staff are involved in such activities as open days, clearing, offering the LRC as a home for fees

collection at the start of term and for Students' Union elections, in addition to our normal professional liaison activities. All of these have demonstrated that the LRC is an integral part of the University community and welcoming to all.

- *Political influence matters.* The ability for Information Services to be led by an articulate and strong Director, able to speak up not only on Information Services issues in committees, but also to lead University-wide task groups in different areas, chair policy groups and committees and to take a broad corporate position in University management, has played a major part in the ability to secure direction and funds and in establishing credibility for the service.
- *Delivering what we say we will matters.* This is a crucial learning point. All the foregoing matter not at all, if the staff do not deliver what is promised. People remember the negatives far more than the positives.

Has the convergence been successful and how have we measured this?

Criteria used for success

The University has not formally set out to measure whether Information Services has been a success, nor created performance indicators by which to measure it, so the success criteria by which it could be measured are against the original ambitions at the time of its creation.

- *Strategic management of Information Services and anticipation of University needs.* This appears to have been well achieved with good responses to papers, strategies and resourcing requests. It is also evidenced in the additional responsibilities for strategies and cross-University funds given to the Department to manage.
- *Turnaround of the IT department.* This was achieved, after initial problems, but needs continual review to avoid either complacency creeping in or reversion to former habits, particularly in the area of communication.
- *Voice for Information Services at University senior management.* There has undoubtedly been more representation of all sections of Information Services at key committees and a rolling programme of prioritization has ensured debate and investment across the department in a way that smaller units would previously have found difficult.
- *Customer focus.* While there is a greater customer focus, as demonstrated through external audits, surveys, academic programme boards and other committees and significant improvement can be seen, the department has

yet to achieve the consistency in approach to users that we are aiming for and policies are not always being carried out in practice in a converged way.

- *Service standards.* Information Services was the first department in Roehampton to establish service standards and to publish annually whether targets have been achieved; it has set a model for other areas.
- *Delivery.* The department has developed a reputation for delivering what it says it will do, but in doing so keeps raising expectations that it will be able to deliver even more!

However, despite all these apparent successes there is one key area in which the department has not yet been fully successful and, although this was never an explicit criterion, it underpins everything that the converged department is attempting to do. That criterion is to win the hearts and minds of Information Services staff. Although the staff deliver targets very effectively and management has secured many resources and gained strategic influence, there is still a tendency for each team to default back to original sections and to something that an individual manager has control over, rather than to think and negotiate holistically across the department, let alone across the University. Improvements can undoubtedly be seen, but it needs a continual dialogue to reinforce it and effective communication and reinforcement of cross-departmental messages remains a key issue. Until this is achieved the converged department will not operate at excellent levels.

Convergence at Roehampton has indubitably facilitated better strategic planning over a wide range of issues. Evidence for this comes from the many audits, external assessments and surveys that various parts of the services have undergone in the past seven years. The influence of the various areas has grown as a result of convergence, but along with that is awareness that such a wide convergence can be seen and resented by others as a powerful voice, with too much knowledge and being too expensive. One example of this is the impact of organizational change on perceptions. At the time Information Services was created its budget and staff numbers was broadly equivalent to each of the then faculties and was not perceived as a problem. However, once the organization moved to eight schools, each of which had much smaller budgets, and the Registrar's area was broken up on the administration side, the Information Services budget became the exception rather than the rule. It had the largest budget and staff, and began to be questioned on those grounds, rather than being judged merely on cost effective service provision. During the period to 2004 when there have been champions in the senior team, this has not presented any significant problem, but now that they have all moved on or retired, and there is not yet an evident champion in the Executive, an opportunity has been created, which may affect the composition of the department, or even its very future.

There has been no formal evaluation of the impact of Information Services, but it is intended that there will be an ongoing evaluation of all academic support areas. However, during the change from faculties to schools, Information Services led an analysis of each school plan and its potential impact on our services. A converged team met with each school, which provided a very positive informal evaluation of services and clarified expectations.

Is convergence here to stay?

For the foreseeable future Roehampton will continue to have an integrated Information Services approach and in terms of what has been delivered there would be no reason to disband it. However, a new University management structure could lead to changes in the actual composition of Information Services and could affect the role and influence that it has been able to have in the past seven years.

From our perspective there is probably a point beyond which reductions in staff would make a fully converged Information Services no longer viable, as the economies of scale and flexibility that are essential ingredients of our converged service would no longer be possible. During budget discussions in 2003–4 the Information Services management team looked at a range of future management models in the event of a need to reduce costs further. The most logical option if the department were to de-converge would be to break it down not back into the original eight units, but into four or five larger ones, each providing some elements of a converged service under a pro-vice-chancellor type post. Within Roehampton this would bring it more into line with other academic support areas in terms of size and budget, and given the strategies that are in place could make a coherent framework for the future.

What makes for successful convergence?

From the perspective of the Roehampton experience the following have been very important:

- a champion at the highest levels, even where the Director is a member of senior groups
- a strong Director and Deputies who are able to represent the departmental position holistically
- peer recognition at Director level and credibility at the strategic level

- single location, while not essential, is tremendously helpful
- clear organizational strategies
- quick wins and clear targets to achieve and visible problems to resolve
- flexible staff
- goodwill and trust from University management in the professional groups involved.

A list of the ideal characteristics of the head of the converged service was created by the then Vice-Chancellor with the Director of Information Services in July 2004 and the order reflects the priority given by the Vice-Chancellor to each point:

- a flexible leadership style
- strategic thinking ability
- a corporate and holistic approach
- a 'political' ability
- professional and personal credibility
- toughness and strength of character
- communication skills
- a 'can do' approach.

Roehampton University has been an ideal place to develop a converged Information Services over the past seven years. A strategically focused and supportive Vice-Chancellor and a University without the trappings of too much previous investment provided the Directorate with a 'green field' site to develop and opportunities to problem-solve were plentiful. A corporate, University-wide and strategic approach to solutions has often been possible, and in some cases even requested by the academic staff, as in the case of introducing centralized PC replacement. It has been an exciting opportunity and a challenge to lead the development of Information Services and to raise awareness of the potential of a converged service within this phase of Roehampton University's development.

11

The place of useful learning: convergence at the University of Strathclyde

Derek Law

Background

The University of Strathclyde was founded in 1796 to be 'the place of useful learning', a mission statement it still embraces today and which applies just as much to the more recent lessons of convergence as to any instruction given to students.

While useful to take the time to reflect back on a decade of what seems – and has been – a journey of continuous change, it is sometimes difficult to reconstruct the sequence of events, the motivations and sometimes the logic in what has happened. This is compounded by the fact that many of the original players have left the scene, moving on, moving up or moving out and leaving a faded and incomplete corporate memory. This author has noted elsewhere the tendency for institutions to (re)write their history in terms of principled and timely decision-making, rather than the somewhat grimmer pragmatic institutional politics which in reality usually drives change (Law, 2004). In Strathclyde, as elsewhere, many of the new structures described coincided with someone being dissatisfied with their current lot and seeking to move in new directions, while others reflect a wish to change what was seen as an under-performing or inappropriate current system. What follows then is an attempt to reconstruct the last decade at Strathclyde as seen by the survivors.

At the outset it should be noted that one of the classic absolute requirements for success is a supportive management. Strathclyde was fortunate in that it possessed a Senior Vice-Chancellor in Sir John Arbuthnott, who was much involved in a range of national initiatives and committees from JISC to Dearing. In that capacity he was determined that his own local institution should practise what his national committees preached. As with many such leaders, his skill was to give others the space – and sometimes the resources – to fulfil their own ambitions. As a very first step, Senate, one suspects with no great understanding, was persuaded to agree to the following precepts: to provide a set of institutional goals that can be made sufficiently explicit at a level of detail that can be used for process redesign, to provide adequate pump-priming investment as a priority and to focus on and implement information standards.

Or perhaps they did understand that this was a framework to allow a radical re-think and redesign not just of academic support services, but of the whole framework of teaching and learning, and increasingly of research capacity.

History

In many converged institutions the lead role has been taken by the Library and much of that in turn was driven by institutional responses to the first Follett report. In Strathclyde the position was very different in the mid-1990s and convergence began by addressing a series of computing issues and boundary issues which bypassed the Library. The starting point was:

- the 'Computer Centre' – the academic computing services – formerly part of the department of Computer Science, but now being care-taken by a senior member of staff from the service following the untimely death of the then Director
- the Administrative Computing Service answering to the University Secretary but with young and dynamic professional leadership
- Audio Visual and Media Services, which had grown to be a large group led by an internationally distinguished scholar. It had moved into curriculum design and learning technologies, but the University had no clear perception of its potential and future.

The major external factor was the drive to create information strategies. All three services were integrated under the Vice-Principal, Professor Sherwood, but overseen on a managerial basis by Nigel Kay who had been given additional responsibility for the JISC-inspired information strategy development.

In an effort to provide academic involvement and buy-in there was inevitably a representative committee. This was called the IT Policy, Strategy, Research Group (ITPSRG), which at that time did very little policy, strategy or research, choosing to focus on immediate operational matters and budgets only. In a technological university such a committee inevitably attracted members with very decided views about the future of computing and the competence of its service providers. In an effort to recover the strategic role the committee was split into two and ITPSRG was replaced by the Information Strategy Advisory Group (ISAG) and Information Technology Advisory Group (ITAG). In practice, this was not a great help, since faculties tended to nominate the same individual to both committees and as a result their agendas blurred.

On the e-learning front everyone was concerned that this was an attempt to get rid of academics from the classroom and cut costs. A few brave and honest souls recognized that this might be part of the solution to the problem of having academics in the classroom. No one understood what an information strategy was and as such at best scorned any overtures to become involved and at worst tried positively to block the efforts of Sherwood and Kay.

In sum, the senior management of Strathclyde had recognized the arrival of a quite new world, had reacted as best it could and in positive ways, had created a new structure to address this and waited benignly to watch the backwoodsmen grapple with it all. In Strathclyde the post of vice-principal is rotational and its tenure brief. There was a need for swift and early success if the new structure was to be embedded.

Initial Successes

For some time Strathclyde had experimented with new learning models. Successes in the national Teaching and Learning Technology Programme (TLTP) and its local successor Teaching and Learning Methods Initiative (TLMI) and then the Use of MANs initiative championed by the Scottish Higher Education Funding Council (SHEFC) led to the creation of the small Centre for Educational Systems (CES), under Kay's direction. Initially it raised tensions with existing departments who saw this as their 'turf'. But rapid success and external funding for two projects, the Clyde Virtual University and the Virtual First Year Experience, demonstrated that CES was undertaking new roles rather than competing for existing ones. These successes put Strathclyde in the van but lack of institutional chutzpah and hard cash saw them sink back into the pack. However, through CES, IT skills for all students moved well up the institutional priority list and in the process of introducing new courses built a successful partnership with the Centre for Academic Practice.

The relationship between academic computing and corporate computing is, in many institutions, a fraught one and certainly one for which there is no standard solution. In Strathclyde, not only were the two brought together, but members of the administration are seconded to IT Services working teams in order to deal with the development and maintenance of each major module of the corporate system. Partly as a result, the IT service has achieved the grail of a common and standard networking strategy. At a very early stage a single networking team was created. The new group immediately began work on an integrated networking strategy. Through a combination of good fortune and hard work a pioneering deal was struck with NTL, after lengthy negotiation and while that company was still expanding. In short the company provided a 'free' network upgrade in return for all University telephone traffic, including that from student halls of residence. This saved the University several million pounds in capital investment and persuaded Barclay Knapp, the then owner of NTL, to invest in a new technology institute. This was the first example of the new structure not only delivering measurable financial benefit from convergence, but also developing a specific beneficial partnership with part of the academic community.

The second phase

These initial successes had shown that the new structure could deliver substantial benefit. The coincidental timing of the retirement of the Librarian and of Professor Sherwood as Vice-Principal allowed the University to make a single senior external appointment as Librarian and Director of Information Strategy. Importantly the post-holder (and author of this chapter) sits on the senior management team of the University and reports directly to the University Principal.

The second phase has been characterized by several strands of activity. First, each of the areas described in the 'Present structure' section below has been reorganized to a greater or lesser extent. Second, much effort has gone into describing common goals and aims for the Directorate. As with all such activity it would be the Strathclyde experience that the process has been more important than the outputs. Third, there has been a fundamental re-appraisal of the notion of the information strategy. Rather than seeing it as a glue, which binds all other strategies together – a common perception when such strategies were introduced (Law, 1995) – we now see it as responding to the University's major strategic goals and a test against which all proposed developments must be measured. A final if tediously protracted strand has been the progressive move of all the major parts of the Directorate and most of its staff, other than the Director of Libraries and his staff, into a single building. The benefits of sharing space seem too obvious to labour. However the five years it has taken to achieve this physical proximity in Strathclyde has more than demonstrated the disadvantages of separation.

Present structure

The Information Resources Directorate has 300 staff and a budget of about £10 million. This scale is important and has been a key factor in allowing some of the projects described here to happen. One of the mantras of the Directorate is that 'we can do anything we want with our resources – but not everything'.

The Directorate is organized into three operational groupings whose names consciously echo their distinctive role as part of Academic Services: Library Services, IT Services (including administrative computing) and Learning Services. The latter includes classroom support, IT skills training for staff and students, e-learning implementation, management of the VLE and media production.

Finally a small central Directorate looks after budgets, manages internal Directorate committees, communications and the external relations of the Directorate as well as overseeing some of the research. There is a management committee, a finance committee and a communications committee as well as several *ad hoc* working groups. The management committee works hard at consensus building. However, it is our firm view that the knowledge that the Director has an ultimate authority to make decisions is a critical element of success not afforded to convergence collectives. The Director is not *primus inter pares*, but has the ultimate authority to make decisions and just as importantly to allocate budgets.

Several attempts have been made to organize a suitable supporting committee structure which engages 'average' academics, rather than *soi-disant* experts in IT in particular. There is and always has been a conventional library committee. Over the last decade a variety of committees has been set up, which attempted to separate operational issues from strategic investment, none with any great success. Most recently the so-called Hub Committee has been set up to vet all IT infrastructure bids. The faculties are all represented on this Committee and in theory if they approve a project it becomes apolitical and is funded from a top-slice of the institutional budget, rather than (as historically) in competition with the Deans. Although this provides somewhat rough and ready justice it has proved a major benefit in depoliticizing IT strategy.

The one remaining major area of uncertainty has been in teaching infrastructure, where several major budget-holders have had partial responsibility for the converging area of refurbished teaching rooms (Estates); computer labs (IT Services and in some cases the Faculties); the Central Pool Group, led by the Centre for Academic Practice and upgrading teaching rooms; and a vice-principal with responsibility for teaching matters. After much debate and with positive support from the Directorate a new committee modelled on the Hub Committee, chaired by the Vice-Principal and with a budget will from session 2004–5 take responsibility for all teaching infrastructure.

Optimizing convergence

Lessons

The lessons learned are clear if hardly presenting great novelty. It has been important to make the University comfortable with the existence of the Directorate. It has been seen at different times as too much of a threat to established structures, both academic and administrative; too technology driven, with solutions looking for problems; and too large and powerful. Although there is an inevitable grain of truth in each fear, the University now seems to accept the Directorate as part of the established order of life.

Conversely it is important that the staff of the Directorate perceive this not only as a real change, which will challenge established practices, but also as an opportunity to achieve more than the sum of the individual parts could manage. Results here have been mixed – for example a common library–IT service point failed to achieve any real integration even if life for users was made somewhat easier, while the installation of a wireless base station in the library has substantially increased library traffic. But in both cases the important point is that thought was given to how to deal with an issue. Restructuring fails if it performs a lobotomy and removes any requirement to think.

It is also something of a paradox that academic staff, who almost by definition work at the leading edge of their discipline and thrive on change, are library and in many cases IT conservatives, seeking investment in back runs of journals and support for long since superseded or home-made software. As the mythical Professor Quincy Wagstaff (from the 1932 Marx Brothers film *Horse Feathers*) would have it 'Whatever it is, I'm against it!'

Major projects

Student laptop project

The story of the Millennium Student laptop project has been told elsewhere (Thornbury et al., 2003). In collaboration in the first instance with the Business Faculty IBM laptops have been made available to all first year students for several years and the programme has now spread to other disciplines. As of December 2004 there are some 3000 such laptops on campus. However, the ability to co-ordinate wireless networking, laptop procurement, mandatory undergraduate instruction in IT skills, content creation and academically led evaluation, plus the will to drive ahead in the face of significant academic opposition, required the co-operation of all parts of the Directorate in a way which we believe could not have happened except in a managed structure. The benefits are not just in terms of improved pedagogy, but in better use of the teaching estate, reduced air-conditioning bills for no longer required computer laboratories and simplified support for a standard platform. Coupled with the use of WebCT for the VLE and mandatory IT skills training, academic staff can have high expectations of the standard that they can expect from all students in terms of IT equipment potential and personal competences.

Shared system platform

By a coincidence of timing the re-procurement of the library system (then a Dynix product) and the re-procurement of some of the IT systems were to happen simultaneously. It was agreed at Directorate level that this would provide the opportunity to test integration by making it an essential condition of the procurement that the systems must be capable of running on a common Oracle platform, but as importantly working on a shared machine cluster. This proved difficult for some vendors to comprehend never mind accept! But there were several advantages. Typically a library will undertake such a major procurement every five to seven years and in effect comes fresh to the process each time. Computing services on the other hand are likely to undertake a major procurement annually. They therefore tend to have good and tough negotiators both before sale and after sale. Certainly that proved an advantage in this case. In addition it has proved much easier to link the Oracle based information systems to both student records and administrative systems and to the VLE.

Research support

In the research area things have proved more difficult. Increasingly we feel we understand the teaching and learning process and what we can contribute. Good relations with student representatives have brought closer links at a time when traditional library use is in slow decline. In research parallel developments have distanced us from research staff and the research process. Increasingly large sums are spent in supporting research but these tend to go on infrastructure, whether high speed networks or electronic journal subscriptions. Research is then increasingly dependent on such infrastructure but the users are increasingly remote, having little need of support or else seeking services we cannot deliver – typically complaining about their inability to use services such as journals off-campus, thanks to the inanity of current licensing arrangements.

However the convergence of Open Access initiatives, institutional repository technology and the approach of the Research Assessment Exercise have allowed us to re-engage with the research community to explore how more direct support from the Directorate as a whole can reduce research support and administration to allow research staff more time at the bench or in the archives.

Making progress forwards

A host of other projects has been taken forward:

- Library Services and Learning Services share information skills training.
- The Digital Library is part of the virtual university being developed by Learning Services.
- Staff from IT Services, Learning Services and the Centre for Digital Library Research (CDLR) are all supporting the Engineering Faculty in its major JISC-funded e-learning project.
- IT Services and Learning Services have developed a new real-time equipment booking system with online fault diagnosis and an asset management register to link to the room booking system.
- IT Services and Learning Services have developed special needs support in IT use.

Now it is perhaps true that none of these require a converged structure to make progress. However, the view at Strathclyde is that the sheer volume of project-based development, the intricate cross links and the need to prioritize in the interests of the University rather than the interests of the department have benefited from convergence. Almost as importantly a critical success factor, we believe, has been the fact that the Head of the Directorate sits at the senior management table and is an information professional – a chief information officer – rather than acting through a pro-vice-chancellor with an academic background.

Making progress backwards

Perhaps curiously the biggest disadvantage has been in sometimes being too far ahead of the game. The Laptop Project and the decision to install a very high-speed backbone (ten gigabit) were forced through subversively and/or in the face of stout academic opposition, although with hindsight the decisions are accepted as correct. Early leadership and progress in e-learning and institutional information management were lost or vitiated by a failure to persuade a large enough constituency that these were of any value and should be translated into what have become virtual learning environments and institutional repositories. As a result several different standards for both now operate on campus. More generally we have failed to persuade the institution that IT is not an extraneous layer, but that it is the catalyst for re-engineering. Nor have we won the argument that the use of IT should be demonstrably cost effective and become a natural part of every member of staff's and student's skill set. Progress has been made on each of those, but not as much as might be wished.

Commitment to convergence

Perhaps the biggest gain from convergence has been the ability to focus: to focus thinking, to focus resource and to focus staff interest. As major new national and international developments and initiatives come along it is possible not only to respond to them but perhaps more importantly to help set the University agenda. It is an unashamed luxury to have space for staff to be detached from the day-to-day in order to think about the future. It allows time and space to establish a shared mission, common attitudes and ambitions and to develop new approaches and importantly to seek external funding to do many of the things we wish. It has most successfully allowed us to develop a holistic approach to teaching in which all of the resources of the Directorate are exploited. Working closely with the student union it has allowed us to start from the student not the technology and to focus on the student experience. Now that the development of teaching is well in hand we have set up a group to look at the research experience. For good or ill, we are directly and heavily involved in the development of learning; the opposite is true of research. The more we invest in hi-tech infrastructure with staggeringly long mean times between failures, the more we invest in electronic resources and the more we develop web pages and FAQs, the less contact we have with researchers, to the point where our very success may appear to make us irrelevant. We are therefore working with a group of academics to reconsider how we can again be seen to be engaged in and relevant to the research process. The management group of the Directorate also spends time regularly reviewing how we relate to the University mission and how we can help to deliver it. And of course we continue to work on demonstrating value for money.

Strathclyde was an early adopter of convergence and when given the opportunity chose to strengthen that commitment. Its structure and methods are no doubt idiosyncratic, but there does seem to be a view that we would neither wish to go back to an un-converged state, nor consider that we have achieved some form of perfection. We believe that a decade into the new era we are probably still at a fairly primitive state of evolution but that we are evolving and will continue to do so, having demonstrated substantial gains to the University.

References

Law, D. (1995) Fine Nets and Stratagems: information strategies and the political process. In *Proceedings of the Ninth Annual Computers in Libraries Conference*, Oxford, Learned Information.

Law, D. (2004) Review of: Oyston, Edward, Centred on Learning: academic case studies of learning centre development, *Library Review*, **53** (6), 332–3.

Thornbury, H. et al. (2003) Case study: the University of Strathclyde in Glasgow. In Brown, D., *Ubiquitous Computing*, Boston, Anker.

12

Convergence at Surrey University

Tom Crawshaw

Brief description of the institution

The forerunner of the University of Surrey, the Battersea Polytechnic Institute was founded in 1891 and grew in size and reputation until in 1956 it was renamed Battersea College of Technology. In the 1960s, along with other colleges of advanced technology, the College became a university awarding its own degrees and completed a move to a green-field site in Guildford in 1970. There are now over 90,000 graduates of the University working in all parts of the world.

Programmes in science and technology have gained widespread recognition and the University also boasts flourishing programmes in dance and music, social sciences, management, languages and law. Surrey University has been awarded nine 'excellent' ratings for teaching quality, in business and management, education, economics, music, physics, electronic engineering, psychology, civil engineering and materials technology, but remains fundamentally 'research-led'.

The University is organized into eight academic schools and a number of support and administrative units. The main operational management group is the Executive Board, chaired by the Vice Chancellor and also comprising the Deputy Vice-Chancellor, pro-vice-chancellors, heads of schools, the Academic Registrar and the Directors of Finance, Corporate Services and External Academic Relationships. The reporting line for Information Services is through the Deputy Vice-Chancellor.

Several sub-committees of the Executive Board exist to oversee strategy and operations of the various parts of the University. These include Information Services Committee, which has sub-committees for IT Services and Library

Services. Academic affairs are overseen by Senate, which also has a set of sub-committees including Teaching Policy and Development Committee, which through the CLD Management Group monitors the activities of the Centre for Learning Development.

Circumstances leading to convergence

In the early 1990s, like others the University was aware of the developments in information technology and the potential impact this might have on library services. Academic services had developed much as they had in other institutions of a similar age and type, with separate heads of the Library, academic computing, management and administrative computing, and audiovisual services. Reporting lines were complex, and some *de facto* management structures were in place, which by-passed the formal structures. Although organizationally part of the University Computing Services (UCS), the Management Information Systems (MIS) group took their direction from and effectively reported to the University Secretary and Registrar (the University's head of administration). In 1991 the then University Librarian (Bill Simpson) had resigned to go on to higher things and his Deputy was made acting Librarian while consideration was being given to the future shape of the service.

In March 1993 Professor Derek Law (then Librarian of King's College London) was asked to undertake a 'Review of the University's Information Services as provided by the Library' and report to the Vice-Chancellor. The terms of reference were:

- to consider what the functions of the Library could be and how they might change in the coming five to ten years; to comment on the range and scope of academic information services provided by the Library and related bodies that should be considered in the light of new developments in information technology
- to recommend a basis for determining the future funding of all aspects of the provision of academic information services within the Library and related bodies, to include staff; books, journals and equipment; to consider how charges might be made for services to maximize value for money and provide additional services (for both internal and external users) through charging for them
- to prepare a job specification for a person to be responsible for the leadership of academic information services, the appointment to be advertised within the next 12 months.

Key recommendations from this report included that:

- the role of the Library should be redefined in terms of the new electronic environment
- there needed to be a change in institutional culture with respect to information
- an institutional information systems (not IT) strategy must be developed
- a university librarian should be appointed with a specific remit to develop the Library on a basis of access rather than holdings
- following this, a head of academic services should be appointed, internally, 'with the rôle and status at least of a dean and with comparable rôle and status in the councils of the University'
- the University must decide 'whether such a mechanism should also be expected to move the library and computer centre more formally together in those areas where services overlap'.

The report noted that at that time 'there is a discernible trend to place the computer centre and library under a single manager' and discussed the relative merits of an executive 'director' of information services versus a 'dean'. Arguing that the need to make dramatic improvements in traditional library book-based services and in the campus network would require the services of senior staff in both areas, the report recommended retaining separate services heads with a dean to drive forward a more unified strategy.

Little mention was made in the report of the MIS unit, which as noted earlier was under quite separate management from the Library and UCS, and did not form part of the brief for the report. It was however noted that MIS plays a key role in the production of information, and therefore must be a critical component of the future strategy.

From the minutes of university committees of the time, there appears to have been little formal discussion of the report, but it was accepted that a new university librarian should be appointed, with the brief as suggested by Derek Law, and that he or she should also hold the position of Dean of Information Services. In this role, the Dean would have oversight of UCS as well as the Library, and in due course Audio Visual Services (AVS) might be brought into the group as well. In approving the appointment of the Dean, Senate made a prescient proposal that in addition consideration should be given to the MIS unit being brought under the same oversight.

In parallel with Derek Law's deliberations over the Library, the University's Committee for Computing & Information Technology (UCCIT) had been discussing and developing an IT strategy, and produced a report entitled 'From Information Technology to Information Services' in March 1993. Although this reached significant conclusions about the need to develop IT both in the

Library and more generally, and proposed a number of changes to committee structures, unlike the Law report UCCIT did not conclude that there was a case for overarching management or direction for the separate units. However, perhaps encouraged by the generally welcome reception the Law report received, UCCIT prompted the Vice Chancellor to commission a similar study of the Computing Unit from Dr David Hartley, then Director of University Computing Services at Cambridge.

Dr Hartley reported in March 1994, and made a valuable contribution to the strategy for the development of IT. Internal discussion of the report extended for more than a year, and in May 1995 the UCCIT working group reported to the University's Planning and Resources Committee. Among other suggestions, the Group recommended that:

- an Information Systems and Services Committee (ISSC), supported by committees for Computing and IT and Library and AVS, should be established
- MIS and Telecommunications should remain responsible primarily to the University Secretary and Registrar, but act within the strategic framework determined by the ISSC
- a clear division of roles and budgets should be established between MIS and UCS
- the Dean of Information Services (at that time in post for just a year) 'should have an enabling and co-ordinating role, advising on the overall strategies adopted by the ISSC'.

These recommendations were broadly accepted at the time, but as can be seen from the following section, changes in policy were not far away.

Services included in the converged department

Information Services grew and developed over a period of some ten years from 1994 to 2004, with the creation of new departments and the incorporation of services previously the responsibility of other groups. There were also examples of units which moved out of Information Services to other parts of the University.

The first stage of convergence took place in 1994 when the Academic Computing Service and the Library came together, with co-ordination being one responsibility of the newly appointed University Librarian and Dean of Information Services. As noted previously, at this stage the MIS group, Telecommunications and AVS remained separate units reporting through the Administration.

In 1996 IS was joined by AVS, at that time consisting of lecture theatre services, a print operation and a small TV production unit.

In 1997, following proposals initiated by the Dean of Information Services and a further review of IT, the MIS unit and Telecommunications merged with UCS to form a single unit within IS, led by a Director of IT Services. Around the same time, the 'AVS' group was separated into Audio Visual Services (handling lecture theatre technology), UniS Print and UniS Television, with the head of each of these units reporting directly to the head of Information Services, now titled 'Director of IS' to reflect changes in the role from co-ordination to strategic management and budgetary responsibility.

Also in 1997–8, two project groups were established in support of e-learning and skills development, initially lead by a sub-librarian who was also responsible for electronic information developments (Dr Liz Lyon, who went on to be Director of UKOLN). By 2001, the e-learning and skills project groups had developed into key academic support services and became the Centre for Learning Development (CLD), supported by core university funding rather than short-term project funds. Subsequently, the UniS Television service, which is located in the same area as the Centre, became organizationally part of the CLD, reflecting the growing importance of video in teaching and e-learning.

With the award of HEROBC (Higher Education Reach-out to Business and the Community, a HEFCE initiative) funding in 2000–01, a business skills unit (BSU) was created as a small group within Information Services, to develop the University's connections with business and industry. It was clear from the outset that in the longer term the BSU would probably transfer to another part of the University, and as part of a much larger reorganization of University schools and departments in 2001–2 the BSU left Information Services to become part of UniS Direct, our outreach and research support group.

In 2001 the University's disability support services were transferred from the central Administration into Information Services, initially as part of CLD and then under the Library Services umbrella. Although this move was widely seen as a logical development to bring together services with much in common, it was triggered by the departure of the head of the student support service, which then led on to discussion about options for how these services were arranged.

Similarly, having been viewed as a desirable option for some time, personnel changes in the HR department in 2003 finally facilitated the transfer of responsibility for the academic staff development programme into the Centre for Learning Development, complementing the range of work this group was undertaking in conjunction with academic staff in specific areas of e-learning and skills and personal development planning.

Finally (so far), in 2004 responsibility for the University's print and reprographic service, UniS Print, was transferred out of Information Services to the Marketing and Public Affairs Department, reporting to a new post of head of marketing services. This change marks the end of a ten-year process of development in which Information Services has evolved into a co-ordinated group of three main services – IT Services, Library Services, Centre for Learning Development – all with a primary mission of supporting academic activity and with a strong focus on the application of IT.

The model adopted

Information Services at Surrey was never seen as a fully merged service with no visible separation between traditional disciplines. Rather, the aim was to achieve an increased level of co-operation and joint activity, and to spread good practice where this existed. The model of convergence adopted was also driven, as may often be the case, by practical matters such as campus layout, buildings occupied, HR issues and opportunities. Soon after the initial formation of Information Services, 'Follett funding' allowed Surrey to re-house Computing Services into a new building, thereby allowing Library Services to expand in space terms but also to dramatically improve Library IT facilities. There was thus never the impetus to merge IT and library staff into a single team, which the introduction of a single learning centre may engender.

The management and oversight of Information Services has also changed with the developing structure of the University. Initially the head of the service reported to the Vice Chancellor and was designated 'University Librarian and Dean of Information Services', the principal appointment being as Librarian. Over time, the constituent services have acquired their own senior grade heads, and the head of the combined service became 'Director of IS'. With the creation of a Deputy Vice-Chancellor in 2002, the reporting line also changed from vice-chancellor to deputy vice-chancellor, and is now effectively 'Model 2'.

Experience and lessons learned

The changes which have taken place over ten years have been a combination of planned development and opportunism. Many have been driven by the staff in post at the time, and their interests and personalities. Overarching this has been the initial set of goals as described earlier and the emerging strategy of the University. Mergers and transfers of whole sections (both into and from IS) have generally been achieved by discussion with senior staff first but followed up by widespread consultation with staff within the services and from the user community. There has been virtually no resistance from staff of any service to convergence nor to working more closely with colleagues in other parts of IS, and generally the benefits have been acknowledged and the changes welcomed. It is likely that the IT-related changes in the Library would have taken place without convergence in any case, but the existence of Information Services has helped to oil wheels and remove obstacles. However, there is no doubt that the more controversial and potentially difficult changes in the old Computing Services and MIS areas would have been more problematic without the umbrella IS organization combined with strong support from the senior university management.

Partly because of the nature of the relationship and the retention of some geographical separation, the possibility of a clash of professional Library and IT cultures has been avoided. Library staff have developed enormously in IT skills and have been selected in many cases with potential developments in electronic resources or services in mind. The more interesting developments are now seen as those between on the one hand learning support staff in CLD and on the other IT Services and Library Services.

Judged by the University's senior decision-makers the process of convergence is seen as having been beneficial to the development of both library and IT services, and for the emergence of a new support and development service for learning and teaching (CLD). Obviously the improvement in library IT has been one of the most visible achievements, and this has been facilitated by the converged service (IT Services maintains and supports all staff and student IT in the Library). The University's first forays into the world wide web were the result of a joint project involving Library and IT staff, a process made easier by the common structure. A major collaborative development has been the University-wide VLE, which has been a result of close co-operation between IT Services and Centre for Learning Development, and more recently Library Services. There has not been a formal assessment of the impact of convergence, although surveys and reviews have generally applauded the new developments and services introduced since convergence.

Like most organizations, universities develop and change with changing needs and strategies. There is therefore every reason for reviewing the structure of support services regularly, if not too frequently. At Surrey, convergence achieved over eight to ten years some essential structural, technical and human resource changes, which might have been difficult otherwise. Whether the current structure will remain appropriate in the future is open to conjecture, and in my view there is no 'best' structure – universities must chose what is perceived to be right at the time.

Success in convergence may be difficult to measure and there is probably no single factor that will ensure success – the expectations and goals set out prior to the creation of Information Services at Surrey have been achieved by a combination of a willingness of the majority of staff to participate in strategic thinking and to accept change, combined with the presence of a number of very dynamic, innovative and forward thinking people.

The characteristics required in the head of the converged service depend to a large extent on what is expected of the convergence – if there are major structural problems to be overcome then tenacity, political savoir-faire and HR skills will be more important than the technical understanding which might be needed if the structure and people are right but the IT strategy is defective.

Other observations

Any period of change can be both exciting and at times demoralizing. Universities have taken on board over the last 10–15 years the need to develop information services to reflect the changes in learning styles, IT, electronic information and so on. It is probably true that to respond to changing needs collaboration between the constituent services is essential, but convergence and merger are arguably just two points on a spectrum of collaborative activity. The will to work together and not to be precious about traditions or territory is more important than any formal structure.

13

Swansea University: successful convergence?

Christopher West

In many ways, Swansea is a typical UK university. It has an average number of students (10,123 FTE as of 2003) and like most pre-1992 UK universities Swansea offers a wide range of subject areas, from French to physics and from engineering to economics. There is a long-standing commitment to research excellence in all of the subject areas studied at the University.

Like many UK universities, Swansea has a merged library and computing service. The latest published 2002–3 edition of the *SCONUL Annual Library Statistics* showed that 68 out of 139 respondents were either a merged or a joint management service, or a variant on these (SCONUL, 2004, 10–13). Swansea *is* unusual, however, in the extent to which library and computing services have been merged since 1997. It clearly matches the *Model 3* categorization in this group of case studies (see Chapter 1, p. 5). There has been a significant level of service integration in a number of areas, along with corresponding and radical re-definitions of staff roles.

This case study will review the change process that led to the merging of library and computing services at Swansea. It will also consider the local and more general factors that underpin the delivery of a converged service, along with customer reaction to the service.

Library & Information Services at Swansea University

Although the library and computing service at Swansea was organizationally merged in 1996 to form Library & Information Services (LIS), the full merging of services and management only took place during the summer of 1997. Since then, a heavily converged service has been in operation. Apart from a relatively small number of staff in three specialist branch libraries, all library and computing staff are based in the same building. There is a single management and administrative team and a unified team for front-of-house services, led by a Head of Public Services.

What led to convergence at Swansea?

The change process that created a converged service at Swansea was driven by a mix of local and broader factors. As with all organizational change, there was an element of personality influences, historical baggage and opportunism. Although these are important factors, it is sometimes easy to exaggerate their influence. From the safe distance of a decade, it is easier to see the influence of broader factors like UK higher education (HE) policy and major technological changes.

Broader influences

Follett and Fielden

As in other UK universities, the Follett report (Joint Funding Councils' Libraries Review Group, 1993) had a significant impact on the process of convergence at Swansea. On re-reading the Report, despite its wide-ranging remit and its beneficial impact on the development of HE libraries and information services, there are few explicit comments and no blueprints for converged services. In many ways, the Follett report was recognizing a trend that was already under way, based on useful models in the USA, South Africa and Australia. The related Fielden report (John Fielden Consultancy, 1993) on staffing in academic libraries focused more clearly on this trend, while recognizing that institutional imperatives would always produce a variety of models for converged services.

Technological changes

Convergence would never have happened without the move to distributed computing. Over the last ten to 15 years, all students and staff in all subjects have moved to a situation where ICT is ubiquitous for their learning and research. Computing staff have had to move from looking after one large computer used by a small group of academic experts to responsibility for several thousand PCs and servers on complex, distributed networks, which are used by everyone in the institution. The ICT revolution has also had an equally wide-ranging impact on the way that library and information services are delivered to all students and staff.

Funding changes

With hindsight, it was bad luck for university computing centres that the dedicated funding stream from the UK Computer Board disappeared just when they had to make a major re-definition of their service parameters. It is difficult to cope with re-engineering service provision during a time of financial cuts and uncertainty. This may partly explain the perceived lack of a service ethos and public relations skills in many computer centres during this period.

Keeping up with the Joneses

Most Welsh universities merged their computing and library services during the 1990s. In line with Fielden's comments, a variety of converged structures were created, reflecting differing institutional needs and priorities. By now, all of the larger and medium-sized HE institutions in Wales have converged services, with the University of Glamorgan as the only exception.

Local drivers

The key local factor in the move towards convergence at Swansea was the decision by the University's senior managers to change the structure and service ethos of computing services. This top-down impetus was fairly common across the UK. As well as the national factors discussed previously, there were a number of local factors, which led to this senior support for convergence. One of these was a lack of satisfaction from senior managers, and some of the customers of the service, with computing provision.

As well as losing funding, the Computer Centre at Swansea faced additional problems with the adoption of a very devolved financial structure throughout the University during the 1980s. It was difficult to accommodate the growing budgetary needs of a central computing service with a devolved budgetary system where departments could choose whether or not to purchase central computing. As a result of this, the Computer Centre faced a number of years of uncertain and inadequate funding at a period of escalating demand. Although technically very strong the service was not helped by a lack of customer service orientation and the failure of some of its managers to cultivate links with University senior management and key decision-makers. This sometimes led to a poor public perception of the service. Increasing budgetary problems led to an un-virtuous circle of lack of funding and strategic direction leading to a worsening public image. In contrast, the University Library, which had also gone through a difficult period of under-funding and planning stasis, had appointed an extremely capable Librarian in September 1992. He took immediate steps to improve the customer focus of the Library service and its strategic direction.

The feeling that changes were needed in computing provision were picked up by the HEQC *Quality Audit Report* on the University, which was published in October 1993 (this was the precursor to the QAA Continuation Audit of 1999). One of the *Audit*'s recommendations was that 'new mechanisms should be introduced to coordinate library and computing provision and to improve links with departments' (HEQC, 1993, 35).

The local process

In response to the HEQC *Quality Audit*, a working group was set up with the rather unexciting title of Working Group on Information Technology. Despite its remit, this group examined the need for organizational change. The Group was made up of a pro-vice-chancellor, the Director of Computing, the Librarian, the Registrar and two senior academics. As part of the top-down process, its report to the University's senior management, *Information Services and Convergence* in September 1994, recognized the need for a significant change in the delivery of information services (University College of Swansea, 1994).

In the tradition of all university committees, the Working Group was slightly cautious in its recommendations, envisaging the Library and the Computer Centre as 'two closely collaborating units' (UCS, 1994, 6) with separate finances, rather than one merged organization. The Library and the Computer Centre started to collaborate much more closely from then on but still as two distinct units in separate locations. The move towards closer integration was accelerated by three further factors:

- *Availability of a shared building.* The construction of new academic accommodation on campus meant that the South Arts Building (a four-storey 1970s tower block physically joined to the Main Library) became available to house computing and library staff and services.
- *Administrative computing.* The HEQC *Audit* and the Working Group Report *Information Services and Convergence* both highlighted weaknesses in the use of ICT platforms by the University's Administration. Following the appointment of a new Vice-Chancellor, the Administration was totally reorganized under the leadership of a new Registrar who was also a pro-vice-chancellor. A key element in the transformation of the Administration was the introduction or enhancement of ICT-based systems. Administrative computing support had been provided by the Computer Centre, although shortage of resources had hampered the development of effective systems. It was decided that the Computer Centre staffing and services should be split,

with the establishment of a separate dedicated Administrative Computing Unit to support and develop all of the Administration's ICT services and systems.

* *Events and opportunism*. It has often been noted that specific staffing events or opportunities, often the retirement of a director of computing or a librarian, triggered convergence. Sadly, a rather more tragic turn of events at Swansea – the death of the Director of Computing after a brief illness in 1995 – probably hastened the convergence process. The then Librarian was appointed as Director of Library & Information Services in 1996 and there was a much closer integration of services and staff than originally outlined.

Understandably, after several years of uncertainty and under-funding, the Computer Centre staff found the events of 1994–6 rather demoralizing. In particular, the loss of several key staff to the new Administrative Computing Unit caused tensions with senior University management, along with fears of being taken over by the larger Library service. Library staff, although they had some apprehensions, were rather more sanguine. They had already been through a rapid period of change and staff turnover with a new Librarian and convergence was also flavour of the month in UK higher education.

Strategic planning

A significant amount of staff time was spent in 1996 on the preparation of an ICT strategic plan for the University. Much of the input to the Plan and the process came from the former Librarian and new Director of LIS. The Plan eventually appeared in December 1996, with the *Tempest* inspired title of *Rough Magic: a strategic plan for information and communications technologies 1996-2001* (UWS, 1996). Re-reading the plan several years later shows that it was the cornerstone of strategic planning for ICT in the University, with almost all of its recommendations and predictions taking place. For the first time there was a clear strategic vision for the development of ICT in the University.

Benchmarking customer needs

As part of the re-definition of ICT services, a customer survey of computing needs was carried out during 1997. Following a series of focus groups to determine customer priorities, the survey was completed during the autumn term of 1997 and was eventually published in January 1998 (UWS, 1998). The survey gave a worrying picture of IT facilities, with only 34% of respondents agreeing with the statement that computing facilities were reliable. There was also a clear shortage of PCs for students and some staff: only 37% of respondents had easy access to a PC. Also, less than half of the respondents (43%) agreed with the statement that computing facilities were good. The main student priorities for the development of services was for more student PCs and longer access hours to these. Academic staff wanted more IT support for their departments and an improved IT infrastructure across the University.

Library & Information Centre

The Library and the Computer Centre were organizationally merged under a single Director at the end of 1996. In practice, the merging of staff and services only started during the summer of 1997 after the refurbishment of the former South Arts building and the adjoining Main Library had been completed. The refurbishment process was the first tangible product of convergence, with library and computing staff working closely to re-design and integrate two previously separate but adjoined buildings. The former plans for separate services in the two buildings were quickly discarded in favour of a unified approach to the whole buildings complex, which had the primary aim of providing improved services to customers along with reinforcing the merger of library and computing staff and operations. The new complex of buildings was re-named Library & Information Centre to reinforce the change in service provision.

What made convergence work at Swansea?

Reading back through some of the journal articles and the internal documents on convergence at Swansea has been an illuminating process. Seven years on, LIS is a well established and stable service. Convergence is no longer an issue and some of the previous debates and concerns now seem remote. Unsurprisingly, a mix of local and broader factors contributed to the success of convergence at Swansea. Ultimately, local institutional needs will have a strong bearing on organizational models developed for computing and library services. Ivan Sidgreaves's comments in 1995 are still very valid:

> ...all institutions will be forced to reassess how all services operate and relate to each other. In the last analysis, however, there is no ideal structure, no single model . . . . Each university must examine its own organisational needs, its own focus in teaching, learning and research, and the appropriateness of its support services to meet its aims. (Sidgreaves, 1995)

Local factors

One building

Probably the most effective local influence on convergence at Swansea has been the simple expedient of combining library and computing services and staff into a single building. Almost all LIS staff are based in the Library & Information Centre. This simple decision has done more to encourage collaboration and to break down barriers than any other factor. Convergence would not have been anywhere near as effective if there had been two services in two separate buildings at either end of the campus.

The power of positive thinking

Another very influential local factor has been the positive attitude of both library and computing staff to the convergence process. Once the decision had been taken at senior University level, the vast majority of both groups of staff accepted the decision and tried to make it work as successfully as possible. Computing staff were also positive about convergence. This may have been partly due to negative factors. Nothing could have been worse than the few years prior to merger in terms of staff cuts, financial uncertainty and general demoralization. There was also the more positive view of several influential computing staff who could see that there were tangible benefits in being part of a larger organization, which could offer a degree of financial stability and backing for new service developments.

Timely departures

Another very local factor at Swansea which helped establish LIS as a cohesive service was the unusual circumstance of both senior managers of the former library and computing services moving on to other posts away from Swansea shortly after convergence. The first Director of LIS and the Deputy Director (ICT) had both left by the end of 1998. This meant that new managers could take over after the most difficult stage of convergence had been completed.

I took over formally in January 1999 and have certainly benefited from this fresh start. Having a new Deputy Director (ICT) who was totally committed to convergence has also been hugely beneficial.

Strategic planning

Convergence at Swansea has benefited from careful strategic planning. As discussed previously, the *Rough Magic* ICT Strategic Plan gave a clear and rational approach to prioritizing ICT investment and service provision during the initial period of the merged service. To build on this, an ICT Strategic Plan is updated annually by the Director of LIS. This planning process is overseen by an ICT Strategy Committee, which oversees ICT strategies for the whole institution.

Support from the top

Having a supportive and ICT-literate Pro-Vice-Chancellor and Registrar throughout this period has also provided a welcome element of support and stability. The transformation of the Administration into a much more responsive and ICT-based organization has also contributed to the process, with the new Administrative Computing Unit proving to be particularly effective.

Broader influences

Strategic goals

Convergence at Swansea was a clear strategic goal for the University, meeting very apparent organizational needs highlighted by the HEQC *Quality Audit* and the internal Working Group report *Information Services and Convergence*. Merging library and computing services had the aims of service improvement and strategic development, both of which were enhanced by the clear thinking in the *Rough Magic* plan. Overall, the strategy has worked and convergence has delivered its key aims. The strategic planning process has been continued by the annual ICT Strategic Plan, alongside a five-year LIS Strategic Plan and annual development objectives for LIS. Even allowing for the inevitable variety of organizational models, convergence is only worth undertaking if it matches the strategic aims of the institution and delivers a demonstrable improvement in service.

Merging appropriate services

Merging all LIS front-of-house services in a single division under the management of a Head of Public Services was a key factor in establishing a converged service. Public Services includes a wide range of front-of-house staff. Some of these have a fairly converged role (some of the Subject Team staff) and there are some who still specialize in library services (issue desk, interlibrary loans) or computing services (IT support). The crucial element is that the Head of the Public Services Team has a fully converged role and can ensure that traditional professional boundaries do not impinge on the quality of our service delivery to our customers.

Additional organizational factors were the creation of a single managerial and administration team, followed by a move to a single LIS budget as soon as was feasible. Of course, some roles at either end of the library and computing spectrums are less logical to merge. Our cataloguers still carry out similar roles. Our Network Team still pursues cabling down mysterious ducts. In planning any convergence of services, it is important to assess what needs to be merged and how this will improve service delivery.

A genuine merger

Both sides in any merged organization should regard convergence as an opportunity to improve services and efficiency, rather than an organizational take-over:

> If convergence is to work or have any credibility, it is because there is acknowledgement and a belief that there can be a real gain from combining the skills and experience of staff working across a variety of disciplines in libraries and computing services.   (Sidgreaves, 1995)

At Swansea, we have attempted to have an empathetic approach to joint working, professional skills and the differing ethos of professions. Measures like a shared tea room and social events are surprisingly important in establishing an effective work environment.

As part of this process, when I became Director of LIS I felt that it was vital to attempt to restore the confidence of my computing colleagues. They were encouraged to initiate and manage major projects and have developed many of the most tangible service improvements in LIS since convergence, including a huge expansion in student PC provision along with a massive increase in campus network bandwidth.

Teams and roles

LIS has placed a strong emphasis upon teamwork, within a customer-orientated functional staffing structure. These can be permanent teams to deliver a range of services or they can be temporary, cross-skilled teams to see through projects. Perhaps the best example of a temporary team was the combination of archive, library and ICT staff to deliver our Coalfield Web Materials digitization project (www.agor.org.uk/cwm/). This approach has undoubtedly helped clarify roles and responsibilities within LIS.

Customer focus

Library and computing services were merged at Swansea to improve service delivery to our students and staff. From its inception, LIS has placed a strong emphasis on defining itself as a customer-driven service. Our main quality mechanism has been our annual satisfaction survey, along with a variety of other ways of listening to our customers.

Convergence at Swansea: some outputs

Customer satisfaction

LIS has carried out an annual customer satisfaction survey for the last decade. There has been an appreciable increase in overall satisfaction levels since convergence in 1997. In 1997, the overall satisfaction rating for LIS was 3.7 (on a scale of 0 to 5). By 2004, this had risen to 4.3.

PC availability problems highlighted by the 1998 computing survey have been resolved thanks to a major strategic investment in student PCs. The 1998 survey showed a negative satisfaction rating of –8 (on a scale of –100 to +100) for the availability of PCs. Only 37% of respondents could access a PC whenever they needed to. By 2004, the provision of PCs had a positive rating of +28.9. PC reliability moved from a satisfaction rating of –10 in the 1998 survey to a rating of +27 in 2003.

The rating for LIS staff helpfulness also compares well with that in the 1998 survey, which had a positive rating of +26.2. By 2004, this had risen to +60.7. Also, it isn't only the ICT-related services that have shown an improvement. More library-based services have also shown improved satisfaction ratings, including the Voyager library system, networked information services, photocopying and the range of books and periodicals.

Tangible outcomes

As well as improved customer satisfaction ratings, convergence at Swansea has also led to very apparent improvements in service. A selection of these includes the introduction of the Blackboard e-learning system. This has proved extremely popular with students and staff alike and is now used in almost all the University's departments. Interestingly, Blackboard has been jointly promoted by ICT staff and by librarians in our subject teams. Some subject teams have also used Blackboard to create information skills modules.

Convergence often tends to be presented in terms of improvements to ICT services. As indicated by the improved satisfaction ratings for library services above, convergence has also improved our library and information services.

The implementation and further development of our Voyager library system was much less fraught as a converged service. Other Library projects have also benefited considerably from input from computing colleagues. As just one example of this, the administration of Athens passwords has always seemed much easier at Swansea compared with the problems that some HE libraries have faced.

Conclusion

One of my favourite political quotations is from the former Minister for Health, Frank Dobson. When asked what he'd learnt during his term of office, he replied: 'The one thing I've learnt is that you can never stop people shagging each other.' Perhaps the converse of this is also true: you can't force unwilling partners into bed. Convergence has worked at Swansea because there was a clear institutional imperative behind it and there were advantages in the merger for both library and computing services. The simple expedient of moving all staff and services into the same building, along with having a unified approach to public services, management and budgets have also been key factors. Convergence needs to be a part of a strategic process. Just as importantly, convergence is about people: the staff who deliver the new service and the customers who benefit from it.

Acknowledgements

I am very grateful for the advice and comments of Andrew Green, Sara Marsh, Tony Ollier and Professor Peter Townsend.

References

Higher Education Quality Council (1993) *University College of Swansea: Quality Audit Report*, Birmingham, HEQC.

John Fielden Consultancy (1993) *Supporting Expansion: a report on Human Resource Management in Academic Libraries for the Joint Funding Councils' Libraries Review Group*, Bristol, HEFCE.

Joint Funding Councils' Libraries Review Group (1993) *Report* (the Follett Report), Bristol, HEFCE.

Quality Assurance Agency for Higher Education (1999) *Quality Audit Report: University of Wales Swansea,* Gloucester, QAA.

Sidgreaves, I. (1995) Convergence: an Update, *Relay: The Journal of the University College and Research Group,* **42** (6).

Society of College, National and University Libraries (2004) *Annual Library Statistics 2002–03*, London, SCONUL.

University College of Swansea (1994) *Information Services and Convergence: a report to the College officers*, Swansea, UCS.

University of Wales Swansea (1996) *Rough Magic: a strategic plan for information and communications technologies 1996–2001*, Swansea, UWS.

University of Wales Swansea, Library & Information Services (1998) *Computing Services Survey,* Swansea, UWS.

14

An evolutionary approach to convergence at Ulster University

Nigel Macartney

University background

The University of Ulster was established by Royal Charter on 1 October 1984, merging the New University of Ulster (situated at Coleraine) and the Ulster Polytechnic (at Jordanstown, near Belfast). With five campuses distributed across the Province, the University is one of the most dispersed in the UK, with some 70 miles between Belfast and Londonderry.

After its re-foundation, 'UU', as it became known, expanded rapidly, rising from 11,200 students in 1984–85 to 30,220 in 2004–5; of these 5500 are studying at partner institutions and 58% are full time. The University's course provision is now the largest in the island of Ireland, covering the arts, business and management, engineering, life and health sciences and social sciences. Courses have a strong vocational element and the majority include a period of industrial or professional placement.

Strong and expanding partnerships have been forged with other educational providers, particularly the local further education colleges, as well as nationally and internationally. The University has a network of strategic partnerships with other HE institutions throughout the world. The University's Vision is to be a *model of an outstanding regional university with a national and international reputation for quality*.

Moves towards convergence – the first phase

Inevitably, the first years of the newly merged University were spent in harmonizing the traditions and structures that the precursor institutions had bequeathed, not least in library, computing and media services. There had been some cross-departmental co-operation, notably in the New University of Ulster where Computer Services had developed a management system for the Library. However, some seven years after the merger, the University determined that the Library, Computer Services and Media Services departments should come together. The driving force behind the new approach was the interest of the Vice Chancellor, Trevor Smith, and an influential Dean with an IT background, Professor Wallace Ewart, in responding to the impact of information technology on learning and libraries and in developments that would help the University deliver courses and support more effectively over its widely scattered campuses. The creation of the new department was eased by the retirement of the first Librarian of the merged University, Brian Baggett, and a senior vacancy in Computer Services.

The Department of Educational Services (UUES) was established in November 1992, when the first Director, Nigel (later Nicky-Sinead) Gardner, took up his post; he had a background in research in the ICT and its impact on society and education. Overall policy was determined by the Educational Services Committee (a sub-committee of Senate), which had representation from the faculties and was chaired by a pro-vice-chancellor. The Department's mission statement was

> to provide value to our clients through provision of, and leadership in solutions to information access, information retrieval and information management problems.

The Director was the sole unifying force during the first eight years of the organization, since in other respects the Library and the various computing units acted as independent units; indeed there were strong campus cultures emanating from the days of the precursor institutions. In particular, Media Services operated as three units, one on each major campus.

There was a period between 1992 and 1994 when the new Director and the Educational Services Committee worked on an overall strategy; though it was never fully documented, there was clearly a sense of purpose in allocating resources for the improvement of key areas such as the University's IT network, the development of videoconferencing and experimental work with learning technologies. Among other successes, service level agreements were developed for library, computing and media. Plans for an integrated management team were advanced in 1993; they centred around an ambitious attempt to create three divisions – Systems, Services and Development – but for a variety of reasons there was no progress on implementing the structure.

On reviewing the evolution of Educational Services in these early years, it becomes clear that there were several major problems that had not been tackled in setting up the converged department. Each service operated independently of the others and in most cases they also demonstrated a different style of operation on each of the four campuses. There was a further attempt by the Director to re-structure the department, leading to a detailed set of proposals in 1996, but this development was hamstrung by the need to reduce the numbers of University staff in that year because of serious financial pressures and the result was the abandonment of planned reform and the implementation of ad hoc voluntary redundancies. There was growing frustration with the lack of progress on re-structuring, which staff hoped would deal with long-standing grievances, while, at the same time, there was resistance to radical change. It seems that by the end of 1996 staff morale was generally low and service quality to end-users on the various campuses variable.

In 1997 Management Information Systems (MIS) was transferred out of Educational Services and merged with the Planning Unit under a pro-vice-chancellor. While this was apparently because of the need for this critical service to be more aligned to the institution's need for access to planning information, there must be a suspicion that the move reflected the perception that Educational Services would be unable to implement effectively the new administrative systems which were required urgently. Additionally the University's web service was developed independently by the Department of Public Affairs, reflecting the early bias in universities of applications towards public relations and promotion.

The first phase of development drew to an end with two periods of special leave for the Director between 1996 and 1998 (after which Nicky-Sinead Gardner left the University) and a variety of acting appointments from among the senior officers of the University. During 1998 progress was at last made on implementing a new structure, albeit for the Library only, which featured a considerable strengthening of the Library systems team, given the growing need to support the electronic publications; Professor Ewart, in his acting-up role, and senior members of the Library staff (Debby Shorley, Elaine Urquhart and John Kennedy) were the main agents in the breakthrough. A new culture of communicating across the campuses through e-mail and video-conferencing was pushed through, accompanied by a heavy investment in the equipment needed. Additionally the post of customer support librarian was created to ensure effective service delivery to a number of user populations who were previously neglected, notably part-time, overseas and disabled students as well as the emerging category of distance learners.

It was interesting that the University decided to continue with a converged structure and demonstrated this by appointing a new Director in 1999, Nigel Macartney, whose background included senior positions in the British Library and the University of Hertfordshire; at the latter he had been party to the decision to move towards integration of library, media and computing services in the early 1990s. On his arrival the University 'reaffirmed that it will continue to seek a steady convergence, over time, of the three services into a single entity, which is able to offer information systems and content via a well planned infrastructure of buildings and networks, as well as support to teaching and research – onsite or offsite' (University of Ulster, 1999).

The second phase

The new Director, assisted by the retired Director of Computer Services at the University of Hertfordshire (Gordon Spencer-Brand), reviewed the whole structure and its aims, and, after consultation with staff and users, produced detailed plans for taking convergence further. The plans dealt with a number of long-standing grading and contractual issues with the idea that improving morale and motivation had to be a priority. It was not radical in terms of integration, but pragmatic; cross-divisional working would be encouraged by a team culture rather than an integrated structure. A major consideration was that the libraries were small and cramped and did not have the space for integrated staff teams; physical separation of service points would continue to be a feature.

The concept was that good communications or interfaces are essential between, on the one hand faculties and the service, and on the other hand, at the campus level. In addition to the reasons listed above, the Director took into account that the Library had just been re-structured and was operating well, and so the temptation to attempt to integrate computing and library strands was resisted. New divisions were created that did take integration forward, namely media and frontline computing support would be offered from a new division, IT User Services, while the previously separate Networks and Systems teams were brought together to form an IT Infrastructure Division. A new Administration and Finance team was set up to service the new department. Aims for the service and a set of priorities for the ensuing three years were agreed. The process from start to finish took 13 months.

External changes then fuelled a speeding up of the process of convergence and integration. First, a major extension at the largest campus library, Jordanstown, was being constructed; most of the extra floor space was to go for the provision of 300 open access workstations (potentially rising to 900) as well as more study spaces, and while not properly a Learning Resource Centre (LRC), this is what it became called. When it opened in 2002, a small IT User Services team was deployed to support the workstations and work alongside the Library staff. A second LRC was funded at Magee Campus and it was possible to design in accommodation to house a materially larger number of IT User Services staff; the shared accommodation and the switch of emphasis from casual use of IT lab workstations to large clusters of machines in the LRCs for casual use drew the Library and IT teams together in a way that had not been possible before. Second, under the new Vice Chancellor, Professor Gerry McKenna, Management Information Systems was returned to Educational Services, followed later by Reprographic Services and the transfer of a large number of technical staff and with them responsibility for supporting all general purpose teaching rooms and IT labs across the University. The department was re-named Information Services, in line with practice in many UK universities. These developments gave the department a critical mass, which allowed a transfer into the Library of responsibility for operating photocopying and workstation support services along with extra staffing; supporting this process was a re-structuring of the paraprofessional staff of the Library into resource assistants, information assistants and senior information assistants, all of whom now have job descriptions requiring some IT and general technical skills; as a result the expanded Library teams are now able to support students better in the new LRCs as well as libraries.

The University of Ulster model

The model, which has evolved in this university over the 12 years since convergence was agreed, is clearly one of strategic co-ordination of service delivery. There is now a well established Information and ICT Strategy and a senior committee to support it, with capital and recurrent allocations awarded annually to fund the main priorities in the strategy. The department drafts, consults on and publishes its work plan every year to show how it is driving forward on the projects for which it is responsible under the strategy and the University's overall Vision. A full-time project manager, reporting to the Director of Information Services, has been appointed to lead on the main information and ICT projects, using a formal methodology and involving users as active project sponsors. Finance, staff development and other management issues are controlled through a Directorate team, involving the heads of the various divisions. However, the structure and operation allows significant autonomy within the framework of the departmental work plan.

Nonetheless, the model is not static, as the experience of recent years confirms. The service is gradually moving to deeper and deeper convergence. The standard and labour-intensive routines of the former library, computing and media sections are declining in importance, notably circulation, interlibrary loans, re-shelving, computer room machine-minding, delivery of projectors to lecture theatres. They are being replaced by support and advice services to users – both those present in the very popular LRCs and those studying or working remotely – by meeting the demand for ever more rapid systems development, by extended hours of service availability and by installation of technology that is both standardized and reliable. Already our learning resource centres are now staffed by integrated teams under a single management and offering multiple skills, covering not only library services but also fault resolution for workstations, copiers and printers. A next major step is the implementation of common technologies and systems for printing and photocopying, which will be managed by Reprographic Services, leaving IT User Services free to concentrate on core software and hardware issues. There are now integrated teams on each campus who support both IT labs and lecture theatres, backed up by a single help desk for all computing and media technology services. The former MIS and IT Infrastructure divisions have been merged into a new Corporate Information and Infrastructure Services Division, large enough to deal with the whole range of development and technical issues arising from the University's growing use of IT for research and administration as well as teaching.

In the future, a likely path of evolution for us would be that a team of multi-skilled staff in learning resource centres will support informal study and research, while another but closely associated team will support learning in formal teaching rooms and labs; this latter role may well decline slightly as there is some evidence of reducing demand for formal classes while media technologies are becoming less labour-intensive to support. The differences between on-campus and distance learners will steadily blur as full-time students spend less time physically on campus so that skilled subject and technical specialists will need to be deployed to respond to electronic and tele-phone enquiries and calls for assistance. New senior staff structures will evolve, with a major role to ensure quality and reliability of service and to plan and implement continuous improvement smoothly.

Consideration of lessons learned

It seems to me that the co-ordination of computing and library services in UK universities is important both for service development and for the end-users. The majority of their journals are now bought in electronic form by most universities; this and the availability of an exponentially growing array of web-based materials as well as the near universal requirement to word-process assignments mean that most library users need to use workstations. For some, the resulting learning resource centres with hundreds of open access workstations are an unattractive proposition but there is no doubt they are well used by students, if less so by researchers who can now access much of what they need from their workbench or office. The LRCs are usually the major physical manifestation of the convergence between libraries and computing departments, but some of the most significant benefits lie elsewhere.

Clearly, the development of a high level and integrated strategy for ICT and information provision is vital in equipping a university to deliver teaching, learning and research along with support for administration. Such strategies can be prepared without organizational merger between the various support services. The real advantage of converged services lies in their strengthened position in *implementing* the strategy. At Ulster 29 of the 79 recommendations in the five-year Information and ICT Strategy were implemented within two years (2001–4) and major progress had been achieved in all but eight of the remainder; I would argue that this success was largely due to the focus of the Information Services Department and its parent committee on the strategy. In line with this, the influence of the combined department has grown, though this is not easy to prove; one example is that the Director now sits on the Strategic Planning Group, which is chaired by the Vice Chancellor and meets weekly and he is invited to report monthly to it on important developments. Another is that the University has met the capital funds required to meet the Information and ICT Strategy priorities each year for the last four years.

There is often much discussion on the structure of converged departments. Radical integrated structures (such as that proposed by Nigel Gardner between 1993 and 1996) can be successfully implemented, but require a determined senior management and support at the very top of the institution, along with a clarity of vision on operational matters. The arrival of major, purpose-designed buildings (such as at University of Hertfordshire) seems to me a vital ingredient for success in implementing fully integrated structures. At Ulster, we are now following a more evolutionary approach, in which the roles of operational units are re-defined and changed; this gradualist policy allows us to respond to the different situations and buildings on each campus, guided by an overall sense of direction.

However, directors of converged services are always aware that they run two risks; one is that their department presents a big target, representing perhaps 5–10% of the institutional budget and attracting comments to the effect that economies must be possible with such a big budget. Being open and transparent on financial allocations and on performance will help to deflect such attacks. The other risk is that the converged department becomes so big as to become difficult to manage; it is easier to communicate with and motivate 100 staff than 300; in the larger universities, such departments may spend a disproportionate amount of time merely running themselves!

Some commentators have pointed to different 'professional cultures' being features of libraries and computing services, suggesting that these inhibit joint working. In my experience, such cultural differences, if they were ever strong, are eroding quickly, especially as younger staff come up through the ranks, who appreciate the development of the new skill sets and aptitudes converged services promote – a common recognition of the understanding of ICT, formal planning, project management, a strong sense of direction, continuing staff development and comfort in working in a wide range of contexts. If a new department is being created, it is vital to ensure that any long-running personnel issues (for instance grading, limited or non-existent promotion prospects or poor accommodation) are dealt with, so that loyalty to the service is won over. Buildings also affect the culture of the service and where possible new or improved accommodation, designed to bring the staff teams together, should be sought.

The success or otherwise of converged services will depend on leadership at senior level; this is most effective if all members of the senior management share the ideals mentioned above and are committed to continuous improvement; no organizational structure can be perfect, so a culture that encourages team and project working is an essential success factor. A sense of impetus or of making progress seems to me important in this context; change in higher education is endemic and academic support services are as affected by it as any in the university. Converged and integrated departments may give less assurance to those who work in them because the familiar structures and professional divides are being phased out, but that makes such services more adaptable and possibly more exciting to work in the early years of the 21st century.

References

University of Ulster, Educational Services (1999) *Report on Review of Educational Services*, University of Ulster, unpublished.

15

From de-convergence to convergence and back again: Aston University

Nick Smith

Historical background

Aston University has its origins in the Birmingham Municipal Technical School, which was founded in 1895. In 1956, by which time it was called the College of Technology, Birmingham, it became the first designated College of Advanced Technology (CAT). In 1966 the College became one of a number of technological universities that were created from the former CATs.

In 1981 the University Grants Committee imposed a reduction of about 30% in the University's recurrent grant and the number of students was significantly reduced. During the 1980s the University's response to this challenge was to streamline its structure and operations, to enhance the quality and standards of its academic programmes and to adopt new technology to support its academic and administrative functions. In particular, in 1984 the Centre for Extension Education (now Aston Media) was established, offering distance-learning courses through the medium of tutored video instruction; a campus-wide local area network for data and video was installed in 1988; the Library & Information Services (LIS) adopted a self-service approach to automating its library and information services (self-reservation, self-renewal, and non-mediated online databases and CD-ROMs); and there was increasing use of personal computers in administrative and academic departments for word-processing, e-mail and so on. Furthermore, in 1987 Lynne Brindley, then Director of LIS and now Chief Executive of the British Library, was appointed as Pro-Vice-Chancellor for Information Technology. This led some to believe that Aston had also converged its library and computing services, but this was not the case. In fact, at that time, the central computing services comprised two distinct components – the Computing Service, which was responsible for the campus network and mainframes, and the Administrative Data Processing Unit (ADPU), which was responsible primarily for the payroll, finance systems and student records. However, in session 1990–1 these two units were brought together in a new central department named Information Systems (IS).

By the early 1990s, then, Aston could claim to be a showcase for information technology in the higher education sector (Brindley, 1990), and the extent of the automation of LIS, coupled with the existence of a pervasive local area network and good co-operation between staff in LIS and IS, meant that LIS was able to start pursuing a policy of 'desktop delivery' of information services to academic staff (Blake, 1991), initially by networking the Bath ISI (BIDS) databases and locally held CD-ROM databases across campus, and from 1995 onwards by developing web-based services.

Convergence in 1997

By the mid-1990s the University was again facing financial constraints. Student numbers had not increased to the extent that they had in other universities in the early 1990s. Furthermore, although the University increased its Research Assessment Exercise (RAE) ratings in the 1996 exercise to its target of 4 in all but two of its units of assessment this did not result in significant additional funding, for a number of reasons. Consequently, the University decided to prioritize investment in its teaching and research programmes during the period up to the next RAE, and significant reductions were imposed in the recurrent budgets of most support service departments. LIS was required to make a 22% cut in its staffing budget in 1995, and implemented a radical restructuring of its staff into teams, while in 1996 Information Systems was disestablished and about 50% of its staff left, including most of its senior management and nearly all of its 'user support' staff. The Management Information Systems (MIS, formerly ADPU) staff were transferred to the Finance & Business Services (FBS) department and the remaining staff were transferred to LIS. At the same time, IT support for staff and students in academic departments was effectively devolved to those departments. This devolved approach was consolidated in 1996 with the appointment of a new Vice-Chancellor, who steered the subsequent reorganization of the University's academic departments into four schools of study, with an emphasis on a high degree of financial and managerial devolution to those schools. Another significant change that occurred at this time was the disestablishment of the Senate Library & Information Services Committee and the Senate Computer Committee, as part of a wide-ranging rationalization of University committees.

Eleven IT staff were transferred to LIS in February 1997. A relatively small recurrent non-pay budget was also transferred to LIS. From the outset we decided to integrate these staff and the services that they supported into LIS completely – financially, managerially and operationally. A single staffing budget was created, but separate budget heads were created within the LIS budget for areas such as the network infrastructure, central servers, the central open-access PC clusters and printing service and so on. Immediately prior to the convergence, LIS was operating with three teams – two teams supporting the schools of study, and a Library Systems/Office Team – all based in the Library Building. The IT staff were located in the Main Building and already organiszed into two groups, supporting central servers and the network infrastructure, respectively. These groups were re-named the Academic Systems Team and the Networking & Communications Team, respectively, and the two members of staff in charge of these two groups joined the Director of LIS and the existing three library-based team leaders in an expanded senior management team. Responsibility for the relevant components of the LIS budget was delegated to the two new team leaders, in line with our philosophy of devolving responsibility and accountability for budgets to those who have to manage the corresponding resources and services.

As a consequence of organizational changes going on elsewhere in the University, in session 1997–8 LIS also acquired an existing post of computer-aided learning officer and a new post of world wide web development specialist. This allowed us to create a small project group to support the work of the University's Intranet Steering Committee. This group joined the existing library systems staff in a new Network Support Team based in the Library Building.

At the end of session 1998–9, one of the IT team leaders transferred to another post within the University and we decided to take the opportunity to rationalize the structure of the IT teams, by disestablishing his post and merging the two IT teams based in the Main Building into a new Network Infrastructure & Systems Team. We used the resulting salary savings to create two new posts, at a lower level, to interface more directly with our users. The resulting team structure remained intact until the de-convergence of library and central IT services in 2001–2.

During the period in which the library and central IT services were converged, both capital and recurrent non-pay expenditure on central IT infrastructure and systems were severely constrained, for reasons previously explained. Just after the convergence, the backbone network infrastructure was upgraded to optical fibre and new central switches were installed, with the aid of a grant from the Higher Education Funding Council for England (HEFCE). Over the rest of this time, however, it was only possible to make incremental improvements to the central hardware, operating systems, applications software and user services. Only limited support could be given to staff in Support Services with their IT requirements, but the schools of study were gradually able to increase the number of IT staff that they employed in order to support their IT-related teaching and research needs. Towards the end of this period, concerns began to emerge about the speed and stability of the network infrastructure and the availability of IT support and, in November 1999, a review was initiated of current provision and future requirements for ICT within the University. One of the pro-vice-chancellors co-ordinated the review, consulting at regular intervals with the user groups and with IT specialist support staff, and this work resulted in a draft strategy statement of requirements, which was published within the University in April 2000.

During session 2000–1, a number of other developments took place:

- A working party oversaw a significant expansion and upgrading of IT-based teaching laboratories across the University, devolving most of the centrally supported ones to the schools of study in the process.
- A Senate ICT task force, chaired by a head of school, identified further immediate areas of concern in ICT provision and recommended actions to address these concerns.
- The Pro-Vice-Chancellor initiated a further round of user discussions, concerning ICT provision over the next five years, in order to update the April 2000 draft strategy statement of requirements

The net result of all this work was the publication, in July 2001, of Aston University's ICT strategy 2001–6, which was subsequently approved by the University's Senate and Council. The key components of this strategy were proposals to:

- implement a major upgrade of the of the University's data, voice and moving image networks
- recognize that the primary budgetary and operational responsibility for the effective use of ICT within the learning and research processes lies with the schools of study
- install a new set of central management information systems, incorporating Finance, HR, Student Records, and so on
- bring together the two ICT-related central support functions residing in LIS and Finance & Business Services into a single entity, in order to clarify roles and responsibilities, and to address issues of understaffing, lack of relevant skills and lack of clear accountability for integrating ICT-related decisions into the University's strategic planning and budgeting processes
- establish a Senate ICT Steering Committee, chaired by a PVC and composed of users from Schools and Support Services.

De-convergence in 2002

In March 2002, following the recommendation made in the ICT strategy, a new central ICT Infrastructure Development & Support Group (ICT-IDSG) was established. The author was seconded from his post of Director of LIS to help to organizze the new department, and 12 ICT staff were transferred from LIS, joining 13 MIS and Telephony staff transferred from FBS. Initially, Aston Media was also incorporated into the new department, but as Aston Media is largely outward-facing and self-financing, and subsequently secured a major EU grant to establish a new television channel (Biz TV), it was later incorporated into FBS, to sit alongside other revenue generating departments. In recognition of LIS's requirements for on-site, quickly responsive, ICT support, two staff (the library management system specialist and a systems specialist) remained within the LIS staffing complement. Furthermore, the post of library systems team leader was funded and re-established in 2002–3, in recognition of the need for library-focused strategic IT leadership to be located within the department and within the LIS senior management team.

Prior to the creation of ICT-IDSG, several of the other recommendations of the ICT strategy had been implemented or initiated. A Senate ICT Steering Committee had been set up and agreement had been obtained from the University's Council to begin a tendering process for the replacement of the network infrastructure. Other projects were also being progressed, such as the final stages of the implementation of the new student record system, SITS; initial investigations into procuring a new HR/Payroll system; and a proposal to procure a new central printing service. Over the next 18 months or so, in parallel with these developments, the organizational structure of the new department was agreed; budgetary, personnel and administrative processes were put in place; roles and responsibilities were determined; job descriptions were written and evaluated; and staff were recruited to vacant posts. The Acting Head of ICT-IDSG returned to his role as Director of LIS in August 2003 and an interim Director of ICT-IDSG was appointed pending the appointment of a permanent Director in late 2004. The new Director joined the Vice-Chancellor's senior management team, and one of his first responsibilities was to produce a human resources plan for ICT. To inform this plan, and to help to address the issues of understaffing and lack of relevant skills identified in the ICT strategy, a review of ICT support across the University has been commissioned by the Vice-Chancellor's senior management team and is currently being undertaken by a head of school. Most recently, the University's E-learning Experience Co-ordinator, based in ICT-IDSG, has produced a report on e-learning at Aston, identifying the strengths and weaknesses of the current situation at Aston and making a series of recommendations on the way forward. This report will be considered by the University's Senate Quality & Standards Committee, which has oversight of quality issues relating to learning and teaching.

Conclusions

The convergence of 1997 was undoubtedly a tactical response to the prevailing financial climate. The low level of staffing and budget resources transferred to LIS meant that it was difficult to focus on strategic priorities, and this was exacerbated by the dissipation of IT support across the University and the lack of a central high-level committee co-ordinating IT strategy and operations. Nevertheless, LIS undoubtedly benefited during this time by having IT staff within its complement who assisted us with the development of our LMS-based services, electronic resources, open-access PC clusters, website and so on. Currently, though, the level of ICT staffing within LIS is insufficient to cope with the increased number of PCs in the library building and the increasing demands from students using VLEs and other e-learning tools. We await the outcome of the current review of ICT support to see what recommendations may be made to help us to address these issues.

Users of the central ICT services also benefited from improvements in service due to the convergence; for example, software applications available under the Microsoft Select schemes and similar schemes were made available for loan from the library in the same way that other materials are loaned; we enabled users to make printing payments or request password changes from the service point in the Library Building, as well as the existing service point in the Main Building, thereby doubling the hours during which users could make these transactions; we increased the number of open-access PCs in the Library Building; and so on.

The designation of a PVC with ICT responsibility in the late 1990s meant that ICT once again became owned as a strategic priority by the University's senior management team, and the creation of a Senate ICT Steering Committee re-integrated ICT into the University's formal decision-making processes. The decision to de-converge central IT support from LIS was undeniably a strategic one, albeit one that focused primarily upon the strategic importance of ICT to the University. Prior to 1996 the Director of LIS and the Director of Information Systems reported directly to the Vice-Chancellor. Since then the Director of LIS has reported to the University's Secretary-Registrar. However, the new Director of ICT-IDSG will report directly to the Vice-Chancellor and be a member of the University's senior management team, and this should mean that ICT strategy and operations take a central role in the University's agenda in future.

References

Blake, P. (1991) University Library of the Future at Aston?, *Information World Review,* (December), 21–3.

Brindley, L. J. (1990) The Electronic Campus: Aston University, *Higher Education Management*, **2** (3), 334–42.

16

The turn of the wheel: projects and politics at the University of Southampton

Sheila Corrall

Institutional context

The University of Southampton has its origins in the Hartley Institute, which was founded in 1862. It moved from central Southampton to its present site in Highfield in 1919 and was constituted by Royal Charter as the University of Southampton in 1952. The institution's historical emphasis was on science and technology, but it has evolved into a broadly based multidisciplinary University and expanded its academic portfolio significantly in the 1990s by merging with La Sainte Union College of Higher Education, Winchester School of Art and the Textile Conservation Centre (formerly at Hampton Court).

In common with the rest of the sector, Southampton has experienced substantial increases in student numbers, particularly over the last 15 years. In 1952, there were 900 undergraduates; by 1990, this figure had risen to 6000; and in 2004 there are almost 20,000 students at the University, with a growing proportion of postgraduates. It is now ranked among the top research-led universities in the UK and currently operates from seven main campuses, all with centrally managed libraries and a mix of centrally managed and school-owned computing facilities.

According to Bernard Naylor, writing as University Librarian in 1989, the story of convergence at Southampton 'can be traced to an initiative in the field of word processing taken by the University in 1978'. However, a whole decade elapsed before the shared interests among the Library, the Computing Service and the Teaching Media Department were formally acknowledged in the decision to appoint Naylor as Co-ordinator of Information Services *in addition to* his existing role from August 1988. This appointment marked the beginning of the first of two distinct phases of service convergence at Southampton, which lasted until December 2000. The second, shorter, phase ran from March 2001 until December 2003.

Circumstances leading to convergence

Moves towards convergence at Southampton in the 1980s were *technology*-led – a response to the opportunities for enhancing research, teaching and administration offered by advances in technology – but had an *information* orientation from the start. A working group on word processing equipment was formed in 1978, which soon evolved into the Advisory Group on Information Handling; it was involved in several initiatives, but not seen as having a central role in the University. The situation changed in 1986 with the arrival of a new Vice-Chancellor, who took over as chair of the re-named Information Services Advisory Group and then 'projected it into the centre of the University's affairs' (Naylor, 1989).

A vision of 'the screen-focused working environment' was emerging, which recognized the centrality of information to university activity and the need to provide a single point of access (on the desktop) for administrative and academic data processing and computing facilities, enabling the manipulation and creation of information by a diversity of users. Although not labelled as such, the description of 'the single VDU screen . . . as friendly to the Grade 2 secretary in the Registry as to the Dean of Arts, or for that matter the Professor of Electronics' (Naylor, 1989) was an early articulation of the 'common desktop' that many institutions are still struggling to implement today. Meanwhile, the Librarian, the Director of the Computing Service and the Director of the Teaching Media Department began meeting informally to discuss opportunities for technology-enabled service developments that cut across traditional departmental boundaries. One potential barrier to progress was the strongly embedded system of budgetary devolution that worked against collaborative efforts.

By the late 1990s, the arguments advanced were multifaceted and multilayered, reflecting the growing complexity of the external environment and the managerial (and political) dynamics of institutional ambitions. In March 1999, the University Management Group (UMG) set up a working party to explore the future structure of academic support services, in anticipation of the retirement of the co-ordinator at the end of 2000. It was chaired by the senior Deputy Vice-Chancellor and its membership was small and specialist, comprising only three senior professors.

The working party's approach was thorough, giving in-depth consideration to its subject through desk research and extensive consultation within and beyond Southampton. Individual members investigated experience elsewhere by website scrutiny, e-mail enquiries and telephone conversations with institutional contacts. They were particularly interested in experience within the Russell Group, but also covered other old and new universities in their research. In addition, they tracked down relevant literature from the UK (for example Collier, 1994; Lovecy, 1994; Pugh, 1997) and US (West and Smith, 1995). They produced an interim report in July 1999, a revised version in November 1999 and a final report in March 2000. The first two reports were informed by consultations with the services covered, the second was also informed by responses from UMG and the final report took account of 13 formal submissions, made on behalf of faculties, schools, departments, the large multi-departmental Administrative Budgetary Group (ABG) and various library groups.

The main external forces for change were again seen as technological advances, but this time coupled with changes in the student marketplace related to expansion, participation, globalization and consumerization through tuition fees – the 'customer-provider model' – all pointing towards an increased requirement for innovative and sophisticated programme delivery in a flexible and seamless style. Considerable emphasis was placed on the need to embed technology in the learning and teaching process and to integrate developments and support among the services and across the institution. Similar needs for sophisticated provision and seamless services were also identified for research.

Internal concerns now centred on the perceived shortcomings of the existing model: the role of co-ordinator (now of *Academic Support Services*, rather than *Information Services*) was seen as poorly defined, inadequately resourced, not taken seriously by senior management and not properly recognized in the decision-making structure. The postholder was not a member of UMG, so the major services were not effectively represented at the top level of the institution and were unable to exert or reflect the strategic influence necessary to achieve the type of integration envisaged. The key internal issues were thus about improved role clarity, strengthened consolidated representation and a substantial strategic contribution, all seen as essential to achieving the service enhancements, strategic advantage and operational efficiencies thought to be possible in a converged environment.

Information strategy planning

In the first phase of convergence at Southampton, information strategy planning can be seen as both cause and effect of the academic support services working together. Naylor prefaces his 1989 case study with the observation that

> The penetration of the Southampton University academic community by electronic technology and the *formation of an information strategy* have been important parts of a process in which separate strands of development are, in due course, perceived to have essential common elements, requiring that they be brought together into a coherent programme and in which some of the diverse members of the academic community realise that a *university information strategy* is something which needs to be devised and to which they ought to give their commitment.   [Italics added]

Although the term 'information strategy' was not widely used at the time, it seems an accurate reflection of the emphasis of both the overall vision and specific initiatives under discussion at Southampton, further evidenced by the title given to the body set up to guide the University's progress towards a technology-based future – Advisory Group on *Information* Handling (later Services). In this context the twin drivers of convergence were the opportunities offered by advances in *information and communications technology* and the dawning realization that higher education institutions are *information-intensive organizations*. The formation of the Advisory Group and informal meetings of the service heads enabled a vision of the future to emerge, which marked out a development path for the information strategy, though not yet in the form of a fully articulated plan.

By the time of the second phase, the notion of an information strategy had been around for a decade and had become institutionalized at Southampton, in that both a formal document and a university committee with that title existed. Reports of the Working Party on Academic Support Services placed emphasis on the need for strategic direction and development of the services and for the services to influence and contribute to the strategic management of the University. These reports did not mention the Information Strategy specifically, but concentrated on the need for the services not only to support and respond to the Research Strategy and the Learning and Teaching Strategy, but also to 'contribute substantially to institutional strategy'. The focus here on the core business and academic strategies rather than on information can be attributed to the Working Party's belief in the need 'to focus on the *academic* process rather than on the *information management* process', which is reflected in the job title of the post recommended (and in the later title of the co-ordinator).

In practice, the new Director of Academic Support Services was seen as a key player in information strategy planning and this role was stressed in the information for applicants, which stated that 'a main responsibility will be the further development, acceptance and implementation of an Information Strategy to underpin the University's Strategic Plan' and then linked this explicitly with convergence by adding, 'To make best use of the information and delivery channels available it will be important to develop plans to promote closer working between the Library and Computing Services, to unify their approaches and systems, to best exploit synergies between them and to provide a user oriented focus.'

Services included in the converged organization

During the first phase, the services covered by the co-ordinator were the Library, the (academic) Computing Service and the Teaching Media Department. This continued until Naylor's retirement in December 2000, though by that time the Computing Service had gathered in related technology-based functions, including first telephony and then the audiovisual and digital elements of what was then known as Teaching Support and Media Services (TSMS). A working party on the future of this unit had decided to separate the developmental/pedagogical and operational/technological elements and place the former in the Research and Graduate School of Education.

By the start of the second phase, the audiovisual and e-media services from TSMS had been subsumed within Computing Services and the initial remit of the new Director was then to lead the management of two large service departments – Computing Services and the Libraries. More specifically, the task was defined as delivering 'a strategically focused, integrated, proactive and user-oriented Academic Support Service'.

However, the possibility of expanding the portfolio was a live issue from the outset. The July 1999 report of the Working Party proposed 'an evolutionary approach to the integration of the services, starting now with the three core groups' (library, computing and teaching media), adding that 'the later definition of which services should be included can be as wide or as narrow as the strategic imperatives and drivers for change require'. The Working Party's final report reiterated its belief in 'an evolutionary process, in which other aspects may be added', citing the experience of other universities that had done this and mentioning specifically the Centre for Learning and Teaching (formed from the residue of TSMS transferred to the School of Education) and the Management Information Computer Service (MICS, which was a small unit located in the Planning Department within ABG).

In the event it was not long before the case for unification of MICS and Computing Services became overwhelming, key factors here being the need to join up systems and services in evolving the e-learning platform into a seamless managed learning environment and in developing student and staff portals. Thus in autumn 2002 those two services were formally merged to become Information Systems Services. At the same time, against a backdrop of comprehensive institutional restructuring, the Academic Support Services group was further extended by bringing in the Careers Advisory Service and the

Quality Assurance Unit (from the Academic Registry). These additions recognized a shared interest in academic liaison and skills development among the services concerned and the desirability of co-ordinating IT, information, academic/study, research and enterprise skills development and of embedding and integrating skills interventions in academic programmes.

The regrouping also reflected the extensive involvement and influence of the Director of Academic Support Services in institutional learning and teaching developments, which had reached a point where it made sense for the organizational structure to evolve in line with the practical reality of day-to-day working relationships. The responsibilities of the Quality Assurance unit were broader than the name implies and included the development and monitoring of the University's strategies for learning and teaching and widening participation. Another purpose in transferring this activity from the administrative support group to its academic service counterpart was to signal an intended shift in emphasis from quality *assurance* to quality *enhancement*. This message was then reinforced by changing the QA unit's name to Educational Development Service and bringing in other staff involved in widening access. At the same time, the word 'support' was dropped from the title of the group and the Director, who then became Director of Academic Services.

The model adopted

The appointment of the co-ordinator in 1988 coincided with the retirement of the Director of the Computing Service, which opened up the possibility of the postholder becoming the single reporting point between the three services and the Vice-Chancellor. In the event, following negotiation with interested parties, the model adopted was that of a *peer co-ordinator* rather than *executive director*, with the role rotating at five-yearly intervals between the heads of the two largest services and all three departments retaining financial independence as 'budgetary groups', each with comparable status to the academic faculties and to ABG (which included Academic Registry and Public Affairs, as well as departments such as Finance and Personnel).

In this first phase, the role of co-ordinator (who reported to the Vice-Chancellor) was intended to provide strategic and, to some extent, operational co-ordination, but did not have formal management responsibility across the services. The services retained their budgetary independence and the first postholder also writes of 'retaining the integrity of the three activities' and continuing 'to lay strong emphasis on the viability and value of the different service traditions of the three service departments' (Naylor, 1989). The role was seen as a recognition of 'common threads' among Computing Services, the

Library and Teaching Media and its purpose as being 'to ensure these threads were pulled together' (Marshall, 1991).

One example of more formal co-ordination was the university committee structure: the existing committees for the Computing Service, Library and Teaching Media continued to play their former roles, but there was an attempt to pull things together more explicitly by requiring these three separate committees to relate actively to the previously free-standing Information Services Advisory Committee (formerly the Advisory Group on Information Handling) as a single overarching body.

For the second phase, the final report of the Working Party in 2000 revealed considerable opposition to the proposal to replace the role of co-ordinator with a more strategic higher-level post of Director of Academic Support Services: four of the six faculty responses were against the idea, and ABG was totally opposed to it, submitting a range of counter-proposals accompanied by data gathered from a survey of 46 institutions. However, the chair successfully overcame all these challenges and UMG approved the recommendations in his report, with only a few amendments.

As a result, the new post reported to the Vice-Chancellor, as the Co-ordinator had done, but in addition had management responsibility for both the Library and Computing Services and was also to attend UMG, as well as being a member of all the main University strategy and policy committees. The existing policy committees for the services were merged to form a new Academic Support Services Committee. Despite the stated intention to provide 'a single voice backed by a single budget', the budget situation was confused by the decision to 'ring-fence' the service budgets for the first three years and the seemingly inconsistent assumption that the new Director's salary and running costs would be funded from these budgets. More positively, UMG agreed a small additional ring-fenced annual allocation as a strategic initiatives fund for the new group, to facilitate collaborative service developments and innovations.

Change management process

The new Director opted for an evolutionary path towards an integrated service via closer working and collective thinking on strategic developments. She took the view that structure should follow strategy – not pre-empt it – and accordingly decided not to rush into substantial reorganization, but instead to build on existing collaborative activities. There were other compelling arguments against early restructuring: a new structure had only recently been introduced in Computing Services and then adjusted following the assimilation of audiovisual and media staff; the prospect of other services being added to the portfolio had to be taken into account; and there was plenty of evidence from elsewhere of structural change taking up time and energy that might have been better directed at service enhancement and innovation.

Nevertheless, several deliberate steps towards unification were taken in the first few months: a cross-service management group was formed, which immediately began to identify common themes and shared objectives in the strategic plans of the services; staff meetings were held at all sites, to provide opportunities for discussions and questions about the nature of change envisaged; and the Director visited Deans, Deputy Deans and Heads of Schools on separate sites to talk through their perceptions and expectations of the services. Collaboration between the Library and Computing Services was already established practice in several areas, notably computing support for the library management system, co-operative provision of CD-ROM database services, a jointly resourced Assistive Technology Centre (ATC) and reciprocal involvement in each other's staff reviews. The last two examples offer interesting illustrations of the different professional cultures and traditions.

The ATC had been managed in an informal co-operative way through a 'management group' comprising mainly the staff involved in the service. Although all those involved were keen to develop and expand provision, their preferences and priorities were different: the library staff liked to provide in-depth specialist help to a tightly defined user group, whereas the computing staff wanted to roll out specialist software to as many people as possible. Tensions arose as these differing aims were seen by the protagonists as conflicting and contradictory. A way forward was found by engaging all group members in the development of a vision and strategy for the service, in which the two approaches were seen as complementary rather than competing. The process also resulted in a unanimous request from the group for formal management responsibility for the service to be given to a particular member of the Library senior management team. The ATC represents only a tiny part of a large group, but shows how the creation of a shared vision can help strong personalities to agree and achieve pragmatic goals (Bown and Corrall, 2002).

The staff review process was conducted annually to identify and approve cases for salary increments and re-gradings, with discussion and decisions taking place at departmental, group and then institutional level. Although the Library and Computing Services used the same salary scales and similar grade definitions, there were significant differences in interpretation and application. Not only was the 'career grade' for computing staff set at a higher level, but it was also established practice for new staff to progress rapidly towards this by receiving double increments each year. Bringing the two services together into a unified management structure exposed these differences to further scrutiny and questioning, particularly after the group was expanded to include careers advisers and QA staff, reinforcing disparities. A case could have been made for upgrading the liaison librarians and careers advisers, especially with their growing involvement in teaching students, but this would have posed serious budget challenges and was therefore left as something to be resolved in the new pay and grading structure currently being implemented.

Success and influence

The distinctive features of the Southampton model have been the continually evolving portfolio of the co-ordinator/director, the focus on academic activity – rather than information management – as the change driver and a continuing debate over whether the postholder should act primarily as a high-level change agent (akin to a pro-vice-chancellor) or concentrate on the more conventional line-management role. The author took the view that she could contribute more to the institution by leading and integrating strategic initiatives than by providing an extra layer of management, bearing in mind the experience and competence of the existing service heads.

The Academic Services managers developed a shared vision of a unified structure, which combined concentration of expertise in specialist units (organized along traditional lines) with the development of multi-professional teams for common functions (academic liaison, information provision, learner support and quality assurance) in a matrix arrangement. They were committed to joint strategic and operational planning and also close collaboration with other services and academic units. In practice, progress towards multi-professional teamworking was more evident in relation to development projects and strategic initiatives than in operational processes, reflecting the priority and attention given to the former by the Director.

Notable examples of cross-functional working included the digitization and provision of access to exam papers and the design and development of an institutional repository for research output (Hey, 2004). While collaboration among the different services was a critical factor in the success of several ventures, development of effective partnerships between the services and academic groups was an equally important dimension of the Director's role, indicated by the wide range of boundary-spanning projects led during this period, in areas such as academic skills development, computer-aided assessment, institutional website design, personal development planning, student feedback mechanisms and student entitlement.

Several of these developments were pump-primed from the Director's strategic fund, showing how relatively modest sums can make a significant difference. Another key contribution of the post – in addition to time and money – was making connections between the various initiatives, ensuring linkages between activities and avoiding overlaps and gaps. The Director's oversight of so many projects and her position at senior management meetings also meant that potential contributions of the services were more likely to be spotted in good time and actual contributions were more likely to be mentioned and acknowledged. It also enabled the services to tap into new income streams, such as HEFCE project capital allocations, which significantly benefited assistive technology, e-learning platforms and workstation provision. In addition, the services gained more prominence in the institution and the Library in particular used such opportunities to raise its profile in learning and teaching.

In the event the Directorate of Academic Services proved a short-lived phenomenon. Within a few months of the Director taking up post, the Vice-Chancellor had left the University and the key Deputy Vice-Chancellor had completed his term. As indicated above, the new Vice-Chancellor decided on a radical restructure, which expanded the Director's portfolio, but changed the reporting line to the Secretary and Registrar, although attendance at senior management meetings continued. A year later, the Vice-Chancellor reduced the size of the senior management group and excluded the Director from meetings, making it impossible to fulfil the role in the style envisaged. The Director decided to move on, the post was not filled and the Directorate was dismembered, with the Library and Information Systems Services reporting to the Secretary and Registrar and the two smaller services moving into Student Services (formerly the Academic Registry).

Evaluating the experience

It is too soon to gauge the full impact of the demise of the group and the loss of the post and the author is obviously not in a position to offer an objective assessment. Nevertheless, it is probably fair to say that it is unlikely that as many projects would have been initiated and completed within a three-year period without a change agent of this type to make it happen. The prime focus of the role was on pulling things together within a strategic framework and making necessary connections across the whole institution. As such, the competencies needed were those generally sought in strategic leaders, but with particular emphasis on vision, teambuilding, flexibility, assertiveness, energy and resilience.

The Southampton experience has shown that creating a post devoted to strategic development can have significant impact by articulating a vision, building bridges and pump-priming initiatives. It has also shown that personalities and politics can exert huge influence on events and often with unexpected outcomes.

Converged information organizations vary significantly in both the services included and the models adopted. All management structures have advantages and disadvantages, but must also fit with the strategy and suit the culture of the institution at the time. Ultimately it is people – not structures – who deliver services and working together depends more on creating the right climate than finding the best design.

References

Bown, M. and Corrall, S. (2002) Assistive Technology Changes Lives!, *Community Librarian*, **29** (Winter), 9–12.

Collier, M. (1994) *The Impact of Information in the Management of a Large Academic Institution*, Information Policy Briefings 7, London, British Library Research and Development Department.

Hey, J. (2004) Targeting Academic Research with Southampton's Institutional Repository, *Ariadne*, **40**.

Lovecy, I. (1994) *Convergence of Libraries and Computing Services*, Library and Information Briefings 54, London, South Bank University, Library and Information Technology Centre.

Marshall, B. (1991) The Development of a Campus Network at the University of Southampton. In *Computers in Libraries International 91: Proceedings of the 5th Annual Conference on Computers in Libraries, London*, Westport, Meckler, 72–5.

Naylor, B. (1989) Case Study: Southampton University. In Brindley, L. J. (ed.), *The Electronic Campus: an information strategy*, London, British Library, 81–90.

Pugh, L. (1997) *Convergence in Academic Support Services*, British Library Research and Innovation Report 54, London, British Library.

West, S. M. and Smith, S. L. (1995) Library and Computing Merger: clash of titans or golden opportunity. In *Realizing the Potential of Information Resources: information, technology, and services: proceedings of the 1996 CAUSE Annual Conference*, 881–9.

17

Choosing not to converge: a case study of Manchester University

Mark Clark

Introduction

The case study will consider the period 1994 to 2004 during which time the Victoria University of Manchester (VUM) has on four occasions given consideration to the question of the structure and management arrangements concerning the delivery of IT/IS and Library services. For the first three occasions review was appropriate owing to changes in the senior staff heading one or other of the services. Most recently, arrangements were reviewed in the light of a 'merger' with neighbouring university UMIST, which is to create from the double dissolution of the former institutions the University of Manchester; this will be the largest UK institution for HE.

The University of Manchester

The University was founded in 1851 and is situated adjacent to the Manchester city centre and has adjoining campuses for UMIST and Manchester Metropolitan University and only a kilometre away is the University of Salford.

The University Library has a significant reputation: the John Rylands University Library Manchester (JRULM) is the largest non-legal-deposit academic library in the UK and includes the John Rylands Library on Deansgate, which the Times Literary Supplement said 'ranks among the world's greatest research libraries, with holdings in many areas that few, if any, comparable institutions can match'.

Circumstances in which to consider convergence

On the first three occasions the opportunity to reconsider the question of convergence was brought about by a vacancy occurring; twice the Director of Information Systems post became vacant, once the post of Librarian became vacant, on the retirement of the Librarian, Chris Hunt, in the summer of 2002.

The context of the discussions on these initial three occasions was that the senior management team (SMT), vice-chancellors and pro-vice-chancellors observed trends at other institutions, including significant members of the peer Russell Group, who were appointing a Director of Information Services. The person in this post was usually responsible for overseeing library and computing services, sometimes administrative computing, and often e-learning, media and language centres within their portfolio of responsibilities. Justifiably the SMT asked whether there would be opportunities and potential benefits for VUM if the University were to follow this trend.

In 1994 the opportunity first arose to consider convergence when a vacancy occurred in Manchester Computing Centre (MCC), which at that time had an active national role but had not been seen significantly to support the internal service demands, which had escalated and changed with the proliferation of distributed systems. The staffing was large and inappropriately structured for the modern demands. Convergence was readily dismissed as it was early days of this trend and generally only teaching-led institutions were following the convergence agenda. There were no significant peer group examples and scepticism about the benefits in comparison with the risks. It was also the case that the incumbent Librarian had no desire to assume the 'wider' responsibility and any appointment of a 'supremo' director of IS would have inevitable consequences for that role. Thus in 1995 VUM appointed a new Director of Information Systems with responsibility for Manchester Computing Centre.

1994–2001

The period 1994–2001 was one of tremendous change both at Manchester and nationally as the role of IS continued to rise; initially it had been the UK university libraries that had received a boost following the publication of the Follett report (Joint Funding Councils' Libraries Review Group, 1993). This was to have a significant impact on library investment, including significant extensions being built at numerous universities and the funding for electronic services through JISC-funded projects.

During this period both Manchester Computing (MC) and the University Library made great progress as separate services. The former adopted a more entrepreneurial approach to service delivery and restructured its staff in accordance with this aim. The Library made significant enhancements to its service delivery through a mix of local co-operation and participation in national initiatives.

In 2000, the Director of Information Systems announced his intention to take early retirement in 2001. Once again the University had the opportunity to consider carefully the opportunity of convergence through the appointment of a single director (it was understood that the Librarian would be retiring in the following year and would be willing to accommodate any change to University structures that was appropriate). The University decided again not to pursue the opportunity and sought a direct replacement, through head-hunters, from either inside or outside of the HE sector.

It is worth highlighting that by this time many universities within the peer group had elected to appoint a director for a converged service – the approach was no longer new in the so-called Russell Group and was increasingly prevalent at that time. The head-hunters failed to find individuals of commercial background with adequate recognition of the constraints, opportunities and realities that exist in the HE sector. There was a final shortlist of two individuals, both of whom were directors in converged services at the time; the person to be appointed had no significant expectation of assuming a converged role. I was appointed to the role, commencing in summer 2001, having previously been at the University of Salford where I had built a highly converged service delivery model.

2002–2004

In 2002 the Librarian retired and the appointment of a 'traditional' university librarian was promulgated with no serious re-discussion of convergence following the earlier opportunities. However, now a new issue had come onto the institution's agenda: discussion with UMIST was now advancing apace regarding the possibility of a merger of the two institutions. The new Librarian was appointed in full knowledge of this potential outcome and shortly after his arrival the possibility increased to a strong likelihood and the merger project called 'UNITY' was launched. The institutions concluded that a merger was impossible and the only acceptable mechanism to both parties was a double-dissolution of the institutions and the birth of a new institution. After much heartache in the process leading to decision day, it was agreed in both University governing bodies that UNITY would proceed; in due course a name was selected for the new institution as The University of Manchester (UoM).

UNITY was premised on creating an institution of excellence leading to a world-class institution arising from the two strong research-intensive institutions; at outset it will be the largest UK university. As part of the due diligence that was undertaken in every area of the University, it was agreed that the IS services (Library and Computing) of the two institutions should be reviewed leading to a proposal for the approach to be taken in the new institution. The IS review was to be wide ranging and was to include addressing the issue of what constitutes a world-class service, what gaps exist in the provision or service scope and what measures would need to be followed to close the gap with the Ivy League institutions of America.

The approach taken in all UNITY reviews was not of it being done to the areas concerned but rather one where it was to be done with their full collaboration and participation. The IS review was established to cover Library, IT/IS services both academic and administrative and telephony. The review was to have full involvement of the Directors of Services at both institutions – the two Librarians and the two Directors of IS; it was to involve members from the administration and academics of both institutions as well as students to reflect the current and future customer viewpoint.

The UNITY review

The IS Review was chaired by Lynne Brindley, Chief Executive of the British Library and formerly Director of IS and Pro-Vice-Chancellor at the University of Leeds. It was agreed that Lynne would be invited to have full access to the papers and work in progress, but for practical reasons noting her day-to-day responsibilities, it was agreed that we would ask her to oversee the group's establishment and its terms of reference and to establish challenges to the initial vision setting. Lynne was to provide a strong editorial viewpoint on the findings in the report and to assist us in making a clear statement of outcomes and recommendation. This report was to be used to guide the establishment of the new service(s) for the new institution.

Media services

The approach to these services was very different between the two institutions but neither had a strong central service model. It was agreed that a central approach for the services was unlikely to adequately respond to the diversity of requirement and there was no significant central component on which to build. Thus, it was decided that the various services involved would be distributed to the individual faculties.

Online learning

The Brindley review considered e-learning and its support structures; both institutions use WebCT as their preferred platform. At UMIST the pedagogy and platform support was provided by the IS Division. At VUM the platform was provided by MC; the pedagogy was provided by a number of groups including a team funded for four years within MC acting as a catalyst to encourage developments

The review group concluded that e-learning should not be a prominent part of its review given the significant planned growth anticipated. It was felt that a centralized approach would be unworkable given that the scale of the institution and faculties should lead a devolved approach. The president (designate) for the new institution, Professor Alan Gilbert, said that he would promote online learning and that he wished to provide strong strategic leadership in this area.

Management Information Systems

The MIS function was integral to Computing Services at VUM and UMIST. The importance of business systems to the new University and of designing an appropriate approach to handle scale and diversity cannot be adequately stressed. An IS strategy for the new institution had set clear objectives and procurement for the replacement of business systems was in process. At merger the institution will run on interim systems derived from combinations of those at the former VUM and UMIST until the replacement becomes operational. The review, although not directly involved in the IS strategy, adopted its approach, endorsed it aspirations and recommended that the MIS function should be fully embraced in the IS service area. Any separation would undermine the proposed approach of integration in academic and administrative computing and benefits therein.

The service review adopted model

The review outcome was, once again, not to recommend any model of convergence between Library and IT services. It was universally agreed that benefits were not tangible particularly in the context of the largest University in the UK, with a desire to build an excellence status, of which more later. The scale of a supremo role would be so immense that it is unlikely one individual could effectively oversee this in a meaningful manner; deputies would be required with partitioned management responsibilities, which would certainly militate against any conceivable opportunities of such a convergence. The relationship between library and computing in both institutions had worked very successfully and there was no reason for this change. In due course, following the review, the Director of IS and University Librarian were appointed. The President (Designate) established the model for his new senior executive team and it was decided that the Librarian would report to a vice-president on the Executive while the Director of IS would sit at this table.

Conclusions
World-class institutions

World-class institutions do not have converged service delivery; there could be considerable debate over the names in the top 100 worldwide and their ranking, but it is the case that these institutions have no evident converged approaches to service delivery. Equally there could be debate concerning world-class institutions and the world-classness of their respective library and computing services. World-classness tends to be related to funding and naturally the services in these institutions are better resourced. Equally most comparisons measure inputs rather than service outputs or quality-related factors, which are notoriously difficult to either collect or benchmark. In another paper it would be possible to give extensive attention to these matters but it is not relevant to the convergence debate.

The scale and structures of the service

It is essential to talk about scale; the role of the director of service is critical; this person must be able to establish and communicate vision and related strategy. In itself the size of the staffing complement under the director is not critical but it is important to have a structure that allows the director to be effective and to communicate. What I believe to be significant is the number of discrete services and their breadth; the director must be able to have full comprehension of this breadth. The ability for a director to delegate effectively with full trust in the immediate sub-structure will determine the depth and breadth issues to a fair degree. Equally the ability of the sub-structure to deputize upwards is also important.

The relationship between the service, its structures and university structures together with the standard of the actual services delivered are increasingly crucial. Quality institutions require all the parts to be working at a similar level; in my own case the expectations of academic excellence of the institution dictate to all the internal parts that they must fully support the overall vision and elucidate how they contribute to academic excellence.

Academic and administrative computing

I state categorically that managerial separation of academic and administrative computing is in my opinion ill-advised and cannot allow demands for integration at the data layer. The synergies and cross-dependencies of academic and administrative computing are high; the nature of the academic service is increasingly dependent on the integration of data accessible from the diversity of administrative corporate business systems (as I prefer to call them). The parent institution increasingly requires certain services to have very high availability; included in those are all that support the learning process directly. These are the student record system, web platforms, e-learning platforms, library resource delivery systems, and middleware and low-level infrastructures to deliver network services, authentication and authorization. The number of systems becoming central to service delivery increases rapidly as information policies determine more integrated models for efficiency of data processes.

Common issues suggesting convergence

Increasingly there is demand for greater resilience and enhanced support particularly with regard to extended hours. IS services so pervade the learning process that there is expectation of very resilient services provision; there is little tolerance from users for services disruption regardless of cause. 'Paying' customers are sadly increasingly less self-sufficient and they expect support to be provided, when and how they need it, rather than equipping themselves with the skills to provide a high degree of self-sufficiency. The demands for more cost-effective support, enabling greater hours of access, are central to the thinking of many institutions and convergence.

The library has been transformed over the last decade by the wide scale introduction of banks of open-access PCs; in many institutions libraries have been renamed information resource centres (or similar). Demands on libraries have transformed the way they operate. The building has to provide a safe and secure place for users to work but the models of work are many: there is increasing demand for bookable group work space, for access to PCs, for sociable learning space, and for truly quiet study space. The building has need to support the technology-rich user with wireless networks and so on, but at the same time it must meet demand for refreshment facilities to support extended hours. This 'learning centre' approach has helped drive the convergence agenda.

Cost-effectiveness has led to pressure for combining the support function to users by the introduction of 'converged' support desks within the library environment. Even for services that have not chosen convergence, it is common to share a help desk environment in the library as an effective location to provide extended service. Furthermore, the demands of the remote user are such that many institutions are building virtual models for support based on either a web service or a phone-based service (or commonly both). These services are increasingly being connected with Customer Relationship Management (CRM) to track individuals and their service histories.

The HE environment

An IT career in the computing services of higher education was attractive because historically staff worked with leading edge technologies supporting niche requirements of specialist users. Historically, people were attracted to work in IT because they could have a career working with technologies rather than with people; however, such opportunities are rapidly reducing and exist only in research-intensive institutions. The massification of access and use of IT has resulted in generic services common to every commercial institution being provided by university computing services. Many HE institutions have little to distinguish their service from another; a prevalent culture arising from maximizing access and support per unit of resource has dictated cultures. It is inevitable that staff operating in 'generic' IT services will seek better salaries and professionalism; in commercial organizations the investment in IT is about quality, security, return on investment, for which remuneration is appropriately modelled.

However, marketable IT skills are being eroded as generally the advances in technology de-skill the support challenges; the half-life for skills is continuously reduced by the rate of change of the technologies themselves. Only in research-intensive universities are the leading edge technological skills valued and demanded. IT staff have not generally been trained for management or endowed through training with customer-facing support abilities; it is for this particular reason that I believe convergence has been effective in certain institutions by 'importing from other areas' skills more focused on customer support, as this has been the emphasis for the convergence model.

Both library and IT staff have to reflect on a rapidly changing environment where skills must be continuously updated; they must have management skills in order to enhance their careers. It is essential that senior staff are central to vision and strategy development so that they can use the associated knowledge to hone their own career skills appropriately. It is increasingly difficult, other than in the few better funded research-intensive universities, to differentiate through investment and hence the strategies for the IS services for most universities are increasingly bland and focus on difficult choices rather than substantive investment. The universities that are achieving the most from their resources are doing so through more effective exploitation of their major cost, the staffing resource of the services, and this is being achieved by spreading the support over more hours, driving the effectiveness through the quality circle approach, and ensuring the skills meet customer expectation at the lowest cost.

There is less investment in re-skilling of staff than is desirable and it is critical that this issue be addressed; many institutions are working through the national or regional community model to provide some focused provision, but it must be recognized that this is far from the cost or quality associated with the commercial courses generally used by industry for their own staff. It is worth noting that educational institutions are particularly lax in investment in their staff skills universally, not just in the IS areas.

Other observations

Users generally know they are in need of support but find it difficult to categorize the nature of the support that they seek, and hence fail to discriminate between various support silos when seeking assistance; most commonly their issues fall between the silo boundaries. Establishing support arrangements that converge the silos, or at least appear to from the user perspective, is a common approach. Convergence is certainly one way to address this issue; however, it is not the only way!

There is no single and certainly no correct approach to convergence; it would be possible to converge a much wider remit of service support areas than those just associated with library and computing services. There are institutions that have created support models, which include just-in-time remedial support for areas of key skills including literacy and mathematics. At Manchester, the Eddie Newcomb Student Support Centre was created to provide support for the administrative, pastoral and similar support issues of a student all housed in a purpose-built facility, which could make extensive use of customer relationship management (CRM) software to track the customer usage and enquiries. It was designed to prevent students' requests for assistance being passed from section to section mimicking the historic data and business process flow of the related services. By investment in technology, a physical support centre, an equivalent web-based support access mechanism and most of all restructuring the administrative support teams to work as a single team, it was possible to transform the student support.

It would be appropriate to ask where the single support desk model should start and finish; what is clear is that the window for servicing support is being stretched and it is only a balance of cost-effectiveness versus access hours that restrains most institutions. In my previous role I provided virtual services using automated technologies; we saw significant peaks that had been unpredicted; in particular we evidenced demand in the early hours as the nurses came off wards and sought to study before sleeping. One group of institutions, led by the LSE, has developed a 'Follow the Sun' approach to service support by sharing support through collaborating institutions using their resources to support each other in different time zones. Much more could be achieved through collaboration, but of course this militates against differentiating one's service from another and as always raises difficult transparency issues of whose costs are supporting whose users, and in the UK context the issue of collaboration versus competition.

The desire to give joined-up help for users by providing the virtual access to support enables a rethink of the model for convergence or services integration. It is essential that 'high end' or 'in-depth' support is not lost for the diminishing number of users for whom it is most critical; in many institutions this would be the research community of postgraduates and academic staff. Many institutions are working towards joined-up approaches to providing virtual support and communication with users, usually through portalization, and products such as SunGard Luminis make considerable inroads through providing an interface that can be customized to the individual user. At Manchester we have our 'Gateway' project where we are looking at providing a tailored interface for every user allowing the user a fair degree of customization and control. The integration of this interface with CRM software, communication software for e-mail and just-in-time messaging, knowledge management (KM) including Knowbots, together with business packages for student records, finance, human resources, and so on, will allow a holistic approach to support for every user to be accommodated. The Gateway project will encompass all the proven strengths of the student centre described, which has been subject to many awards, but will further broaden the services encompassed.

Reference

Joint Funding Councils' Libraries Review Group (1993) *Report* (the Follett Report), Bristol, HEFCE.

18

The non-convergence option: a case study of Bristol UWE

Ali Taylor

About Bristol UWE

The University of the West of England, Bristol (Bristol UWE), traces its history through Bristol Polytechnic to the Merchant Venturers' Navigation School established in 1595. The University itself was designated under the Further and Higher Education Act 1992, while the enlarged Faculty of Health and Social Care was created in 1996 following incorporation of two health colleges. Bristol UWE is one of the largest universities in England in terms of full-time undergraduate enrolment (with some 25,000 students), and a major provider in the south west, with the largest student population and the broadest range of subjects and disciplines of any HE institution. Based on the north-eastern edge of Bristol, the University is also one of the largest employers in the Bristol area, employing over 5000 people.

The term 'Information Services' was used as a working title for an integrated ITS and Library service at Bristol UWE. Such a service may or may not have included some administrative as well as academic support services depending on how the boundaries were finally defined.

Circumstances leading to review

The review of the interrelationship between ITS and Library Services was commissioned early in 2001 following a co-incidence of events, in particular the adoption of an ambitious new institutional strategy and the departure of several senior members of ITS and Library staff, including the head of each service. For ITS in particular the previous 12 months had been a time of considerable uncertainty. This had arisen for a variety of reasons, mainly a combination of changes in personnel at a senior level and changes in major IT systems across the institution. The Library had also undergone some fundamental changes in its management team with the Head of Service going on long-term sick leave immediately following, but unrelated to major changes in the staffing structure, especially among the senior staff.

In consultation with the Board of Governors, the Strategic Planning Executive (SPE, a group comprising the Vice-Chancellor and the two deputy vice-chancellors) saw this as an opportune time to consider the issues surrounding strategic integration and possible service merger. In the interim an assistant vice-chancellor (AVC) was asked to assume the role of 'Acting Head of Information Services', drawing together the strategic development of Library Services and ITS by focusing on the co-ordination of the services and advising the Vice-Chancellor on the most effective management structure in the longer term. The SPE had no predetermined or preferred model; the review was genuinely open.

Involving to some extent the management teams of both services, who consequently influenced the proposal put to SPE, the review covered the following:

- experience from elsewhere, including the drivers for integration and the different models adopted
- the advantages and disadvantages of integration in terms of Bristol UWE
- a number of implementation issues
- some of the possible implications of 'convergence' or 'integration' at Bristol UWE.

Experience from elsewhere

At the time of the initial SPE decision to review the leadership of the two services there was little direct knowledge in Bristol UWE of the integration ITS and Library Services in other institutions and a literature review was undertaken by the Acting Head of Library Services. This indicated that higher education institutions (HEIs) most commonly consider moving towards an integrated model of academic support service when a vacancy occurs at head of service level in the institution's library and/or computing services. Other possible triggers were the creation of a new strategy, a new building or the need to strengthen a weak service.

There was also evidence of more fundamental drivers, for example:

- The increasing reliance of libraries on information and communication technologies (ICT), primarily the web, as the key to delivering effective services to the desk-top as well as in the more traditional 'library' setting.
- The convergence of information and the technology on which it relies (libraries need technology for information delivery at the same time as IT services are more concerned than hitherto with the information they are delivering as well as the technology for delivering it) leads to the boundaries for academics, students and support staff being blurred.
- The continued growth of demand by users for 24 hour, seven days a week, access to facilities and resources.

Many of these factors were present at Bristol UWE, making an integrated approach a logical potential development. However the literature review also indicated that an institution needs to be clear about its overall objectives for integration well in advance of embarking on the process leading towards integration (the preferred term at Bristol UWE; the term merger was considered to be too politically sensitive), as it can be risky, and prove time-consuming and expensive. Finally, the literature review revealed a diversity of models to the extent that almost every example took a different form. Hirshon's typology was used to illustrate these to the SPE starting with the least complex and possibly easiest to achieve (Model 1 in Hanson's typology), and finishing with the most complex (Model 3) (see Chapter 1, p. 5). There was some evidence that an HEI may move in either direction along this spectrum over time, perhaps more commonly in the direction of increasing integration, and that there were examples of changing models of integration or merger. At the time of the Bristol UWE review there were few examples of complete 'de-merger'.

The SPE was interested in the diversity of models within the UK HE sector, noting that the most 'extreme' clustering extended to embracing printing and stationery, chaplaincy and recreation services and that there was 'no single optimum model'. The most common UK model appeared to comprise a core of ITS and Library Services, and a range of smaller services, such as audiovisual, telecommunications and development of use of the web for academic, administrative and support purposes. The SPE also considered the experience of some institutions, which suggested that the small services should be incorporated in advance of the main merger, while noting that the models followed in other HEIs invariably incorporated 'academic' computing, for example support for teaching and research, and that it was not uncommon for administrative and housekeeping computing to be separated.

At Bristol UWE it would have been sensible to include in the review the location of a number of small services, which were dispersed across the institution in terms of organizational structures, line management and physical location, but these could have been incorporated into another service such as the library or ITS, or in some way brought together, without any further integration. The distinction between administrative and academic computing is blurred at Bristol UWE; for example, ISIS, the student record system, is also the main housekeeping and administrative system, including details of staff. There was also strong opposition within ITS to dis-aggregating administrative and academic computing. The aim at Bristol UWE was to provide a single integrated computing service. To separate the two it was argued, was imposing an new artificial divide to replace the existing one.

At this point, March 2001, the Acting Head of Library Services and the Assistant Vice-Chancellor acting as the Head of Information Services (and IT Services) were authorized to consult the heads of relevant services in other UK HEIs and explore their perceptions and experience. These consultative discussions took place mainly by telephone following a general e-mail sent to the appropriate discussion lists, were semi-structured and focused on the following areas:

• the factors perceived as necessary for successful integration
• why integration sometimes failed
• the arguments against integration
• the advantages and disadvantages of integration.

Altogether 23 heads of service were consulted. It was interesting to note that while representing a mix of converged and separate IT and library services, the majority of heads came from a library background. This reflected experience in the USA and Australia as evidenced in the literature review. Although there appeared to a number of reasons for this – salary levels, the academic background more commonly found among librarians than heads of IT, the non-technical background of selection and appointment panels – it appeared to be more than just coincidence but there was no obvious single defining characteristic. This and the variety of models meant that no pattern stood out as immediately applicable to Bristol UWE; we would have needed to develop our own.

The views of this group of heads of service supported the evidence of the literature review about the prerequisites for successful integration – the need for clear institutional and strategic priorities as the triggers for integration; a climate of readiness for, and open embracing of, the advantages of integration by the whole HEI not just the two services; recognition of the possible disadvantages of integration; and, perhaps the most important, institutional acceptance by all stakeholders of the size and scope of a project to integrate two services, and the resources needed in terms of time, money and executive commitment. Of these only the first – the articulation of strategic priorities – existed at Bristol UWE.

Local proposals

Following the external consultation a paper was drafted by the acting Heads of IS and Library Services. Pulling together the core themes as outlined in the literature and the experience of colleagues in the sector, the paper explored the advantages and disadvantages of integration, the factors apparently needed to make integration succeed, and some of the implementation issues that might pertain to integrating ITS and Library Services at Bristol UWE. It concluded with a series of questions designed to trigger and encourage reflection and discussion, for example, does Bristol UWE need to continue to have a head of IT Services and Library Services? If Bristol UWE were to appoint a head of IS, was there a preference for a library or IT specialist? At what level should the appointment be made? This paper was circulated to the management teams of the two services and their comments incorporated. It was also discussed at routine meetings of Deans and Directorate, and Heads. The SPE took the paper and reports of the meetings in which it had already been considered in May 2001. The outcome of the SPE meeting, to which the AVC (acting Head of IS) and the acting Head of Library Services contributed, was agreement to recommend to governors that:

- the two services remain separate organizational structures
- recruitment of a new head of ITS would commence
- the position of the acting Head of Library Services should be clarified
- membership and operation of the IS Executive (see below) would be reviewed to facilitate integration and co-ordination at a strategic level
- the position of the two services relative to each other and other services be reviewed again in five years' time.

The SPE's decision was based on the following considerations.

- A number of the factors deemed to be necessary for successful integration were not present at that time in Bristol UWE. These were:
  — the unequal strength of the two services
  — the lack of a long history of effective collaboration between the services as services, or among the senior staff as individuals
  — significantly different professional cultures each with its own strengths and weaknesses

- — a lack of readiness among the university community to welcome integration
  — that the institutional need for an integrated Information Service had not then been clearly and sufficiently articulated; was it possible to achieve the same ends via a different route or mechanism?
- There were concerns about recruiting a head of IS with the relevant skills and experience in a suitable time frame, particularly if there was continued uncertainty about the future of the services and the Head of IS's relationship with a putative Information Service.
- Both services operated across the then eight Bristol UWE campuses and there was no prospect of physically integrating the services in one building. The evidence of experience elsewhere indicated that this was an obstacle to effective integration with a significantly disproportionate impact on, for example, changes in service cultures and building any new, integrated service.
- The deans and their executives, and to a lesser extent the heads of service, had expressed reservations about the size of an integrated Information Services. It would have been one of the largest budget holders at about 10% of the University's budget with a significant staff and equipment budget. There were also concerns about either service having an adverse effect on the quality of the service delivered by the other.
- Even in the long term, appointing a head of Information Services was unlikely to lead to any cost savings as experience showed that the constituent services still needed leading and managing at a senior level and representation on key university bodies, also at a senior level. Many of the benefits of an integrated approach to IS, for example service improvements and an integrated approach to service development, are likely to be largely intangible.

Experiences and lessons learned

Bristol UWE is an open organization with a strong consultative culture and an ethos of active participation and decision-making based on University-wide debate. Most Bristol UWE staff would expect anything as significant as the possible integration of two major services to be discussed fully with all the stakeholders, especially, but not exclusively, the staff of the two services most directly involved through open meetings, one-to-one meetings, and so on. The views of service users, staff and students, would also have been sought and considered.

What was noticeable to the Head of Library Services and the acting Head of IS about this review at the time at the time it took place was the apparent lack of open and full consultation when compared with structural and organizational changes before and since, such as mergers of faculties, of which there have been two in the last five years. One merger involved bringing two large faculties together on one campus and the other bought three faculties together as one, but across two campuses. By way of contrast, it was known in 2001 that integration of library and computing was being looked at by the SPE but the amount of direct involvement of Bristol UWE staff more widely was limited. Academic Board was kept informed about the review process and the subsequent appointment of a head of ITS and a head of Library Services by brief verbal reports. Deans and heads of service were briefed about the review and, as mentioned earlier, discussed with the Directorate the briefing paper prepared for the SPE. The views of the senior staff in each service were sought by the respective heads of service, but there was little, if any, direct and/or formal input from the majority of these stakeholders.

What was also unclear, and remains so, is the amount of discussion individual SPE members had with individual members of staff from faculties and services at a range of levels across the University, or with executive counterparts in institutions elsewhere. Experience over the three plus years since the ITS/Library review indicates that it was probably more extensive than appearances and anecdotal evidence might otherwise indicate, and that such consultations drew heavily on experiences elsewhere and how they might translate into practice at Bristol UWE. A number of different models would have been mapped out by the Vice-Chancellor and considered in the SPE prior to discussion with the governors, but much of this work would have been completed without general knowledge or recognition. To the University community at large, the decision was taken primarily by the SPE led by the Vice-Chancellor, and endorsed by the governors on the Vice-Chancellor's recommendation.

The difference in practice between the library/ITS scenario and the merger of faculties was not as great as it might seem. The difference is that the faculty mergers happened whereas the integration of computing and libraries did not. A review of the process leading to the faculty mergers indicates that considerable preparatory work was done in the background as outlined above for Library Services and ITS before the decision to merge was taken – the preparatory work was undertaken to inform the decision. It was only after the decision in principle to merge faculties had been taken and endorsed by the governors that the proposals for merger became public and wider consultations commenced.

The management team from ITS felt less engaged with the review than the library management team until the review was relatively well advanced. This may have been because much of the background work was carried out by the

Head of Library Services, and was perhaps compounded by the fact that the heads of services in other HEIs who were willing to be consulted were predominantly from a library background. Members of this group were self-selecting as they responded to a general e-mail enquiry. Some colleagues felt vulnerable as a consequence, which reinforces the need for sensitive management and handling of such processes and the importance of effective and timely communication, tailored to the audience being addressed.

While the review was under way, and before the outcomes were known, Library Services and ITS began to work together at an operational level, underpinned by greater collaboration at a strategic level.

To achieve greater cohesion between the services at a strategic level the operation of the IS Executive was reviewed. The IS Executive is one of a number of executives that reflect the pattern of governors' committees, for instance Finance, Property and Estates. Usually chaired at Directorate level, they provide strategic oversight and support for the area they are responsible for and are a useful forum for the relevant service heads. The IS Executive membership was revised to strengthen the presence of Library Services and ITS, and a dean was co-opted to ensure there was clear academic direction. The Chair of the IS Executive, a deputy vice-chancellor, was the Directorate line manager of both services.

The Bristol UWE annual planning round agrees objectives for each service and faculty as part of a rolling strategic plan covering a three-to-five year span. The logistics of this were adjusted to facilitate joint preparation of plans by the two services and overlap of their respective planning meetings. This was complemented by joint meetings of the two management teams every six to eight weeks, regular meetings of the service heads and of counterparts across the services. None of this was particularly innovative but had proved almost impossible to achieve in earlier attempts. These developments may have been facilitated by the appointment of two new heads and other changes in personnel in the management teams of the two services.

At an operational level the outcome was, for example, a joint ITS and Library enquiry desk based in the Bolland Library on the main campus, shared training and development as appropriate, and greater joint working on projects and service delivery. By the start of the 2003–4 academic session the dividing line for users of the service was far less marked and there were clear benefits in terms of one-stop shop support, especially for students to the extent that computing and library services at Bristol UWE have moved through the case study models to approximate to Model 2, with the IS Executive taking on the role of the 'senior post-holder' or 'director' exercising active co-ordination as identified in case study Model 1.

These 'devices' and strategies have proved sufficiently effective that were the organizational structure and operation of services to be reviewed now, the exercise would probably show that combining aspects of the activities and role of the Centre for Student Affairs (CSA) would be more beneficial to the quality of the student experience.

The CSA works closely with the Students Union, faculties and services to provide support and counselling across a range of areas, including for example finance, academic matters, progression, study skills, transferable skills, moving between programmes and personal problems. It has become embedded as the means to achieving the end, not the end itself.

References

Hirshon, A. (1998) *Integrating Computing and Library Services*, CAUSE Professional Paper Series, 18, Boulder, Colorado, Educause.

Law, D. (1998) Convergence of Academic Support Services. In Hanson, T. and Day, J. (eds) *Managing the Electronic Library: a practical guide for information professionals*, East Grinstead, Bowker Saur.

19

Convergence in Australia

Helen Hayes and Vic Elliott

Australia, in common with other countries, has approached convergence in a variety of ways, with the union sometimes formal, sealed by 'marriage vows' or light touch, agreed on a 'handshake'. In some cases the model has been simply administrative in nature, involving little more than the grouping of the library, information technology services and, more recently, the online learning centre within one division under the oversight of a single chief information officer or pro-vice-chancellor. Often in such cases little or no integration at a functional level has occurred. At the other extreme, under what might be termed the full convergence model, the previous conventional organizational structures have been dissolved to allow a new alignment of functions across former boundaries. A third approach, which recognizes the reality of convergence but seeks to achieve synergies not through restructuring but through collaboration between existing organizational units, has emerged more recently as institutional pressures force change in the way in which information services are supported and delivered. And it is also to this collaborative or relationship model that universities have often returned upon the failure of experiments in convergence of a structural kind.

Rationale

The drivers for change under the banner of convergence, as identified by Australian universities, are similar in nature and relate largely to competitive challenges within an increasingly globalized information environment and to an urgent need to provide new information infrastructure and services. When, for example, the University of Newcastle sought strategic advantage through the integration of its information, education and technology services in early 1997, the following arguments were offered in support of change:

> We noted that the tertiary education environment was undergoing significant change as technology enabled students to undertake studies which are time and place independent. We were moving into a highly competitive global knowledge economy where information technology is a strategic differentiator and where our students increasingly expect high quality, flexible information and education services without the constraints of time or distance. To strategically respond to these changes and position the university for a networked learner future we argued that we must put in place appropriate plans, policies, strategies, structures and culture. We needed to create new strategic relationships between library and information professionals, information and education technologists, trainers and staff developers, instructional designers and media designers and producers if we were to thrive in a networked learner environment.   (O'Brien and Sidorko, 2000, 4)

At the University of Melbourne, where a wide-ranging full convergence model was introduced in 2000, the vision elements driving the integration of library, information technology and e-learning services were identified as follows:

- to integrate organizational units in a way that provides seamless inter-actions and recognizes that there are interdependencies among key suppliers of information services
- to create a flexible, responsive structure that facilitates further change and development as experience with new ways of working and experimentation and investment in new technologies inform better ways to service the University commitments to research, learning and teaching
- to be viewed as a seamless information resource with service delivery that is responsive and at the forefront of emerging technologies
- to be both a support and a catalyst for new ways of managing information across all of the University
- to develop leadership that is collaborative, recognizing that organizational borders are porous; sharing information and expertise to achieve better results for the University
- to achieve a high level of convergence and interaction between professionals based on teamwork, innovation and achievement
- to create a high performing leadership team developed around common values, agreed goals and pride in achievement.

Broadly speaking, the model was expected to be more than the sum of its parts and characterized by greater joined-up thinking, planning and doing.

The practical outcomes expected to arise out of the implementation of the convergence model included:

- an holistic approach to information service delivery and a seamless experience for users
- an opportunity to build on synergies between groups and to realign services in a broader framework
- an ability to ensure that all parts of the information environment were working together to achieve agreed goals
- a user-centred approach across all information services; greater access to different skills and professional expertise
- the ability to move resources to areas of highest priority; and the elimination of barriers, silos and duplication of effort.

At the University of Melbourne, as elsewhere, there was strong emphasis on the need for integrated planning rather than piecemeal strategies for managing information, given the importance of information as a strategic resource and its key role in the knowledge economy where universities see themselves as key players.

The findings in late 1999 of the Information Policy Working Party at the Australian National University, which led to the establishment of a converged division of information, were not dissimilar (ANU, 1999). The Working Party concluded that the University was facing urgent challenges to:

- effect a far-reaching change in our academic and managerial cultures, which will transform the ways we obtain, value and deploy information in the information age
- provide quality education programs through flexible delivery arrangements
- maintain global competitiveness through rapid and wide-ranging access to information, such as specialized databases
- maintain global competitiveness through flexible teaching and learning processes
- foster information literacy amongst the university community
- value and respect our information processes as well as those of others whose information we need in order to pursue our research, teaching, learning and management goals, for example copyright, cultural and intellectual property.

To meet these challenges and the institutional goals they implied, the Working Party argued for structural change. There was a need for infrastructure and services that did not currently exist and it was unlikely that these would emerge in the absence of improved organizational structures. In particular, the Working Party identified certain priority business issues that were not catered for consistently throughout the institutions, under existing organizational arrangements including: integrated corporate and scholarly information services; staff development programmes in information literacy; server support for innovative teaching materials; multimedia publishing standards and support; digital asset management services; information commons; web-based corporate information management; and standard services for desktops.

Given the continuing nature of technological change, it was essential that the new structure be informed, flexible and responsive and with a strong internal planning capability. In addition to the advantages of improved co-ordination, it was also clear that a consolidated structure would allow the University to balance resource allocation and priority setting more effectively than it could across the existing smaller and separate groupings.

Structures

Although the impetus for change remains broadly similar across those institutions that have pursued organizational convergence, the resultant structures differ in kind. At the University of Newcastle, the various information-oriented services are currently grouped within an Education Services Portfolio and their Directors or Managers report to the post of Executive Director and University Librarian. The four component areas within the portfolio comprise Library Services, the Network for Innovation in Teaching and Learning, Technology Services, and Planning and Development. In the Newcastle model, Information Technology Services sits outside the Education Services Portfolio, being located in a separate Infrastructure Services Portfolio. However, the Technology Services area within Education Services retains responsibility for support for desktop services, classroom and lecture theatre technology, and help desk and call centre services.

The Information Division at the University of Melbourne is more comprehensive in scope. There are seven component areas (Administrative Systems; Information Strategies; Information Resources Access; Client Services; Teaching, Learning and Research Support; Systems and IT Infrastructure; and Business Management Services), all reporting through their Directors or Managers to the Vice-Principal (Information). Under this model, the responsibility for supporting and delivering library services is largely located within the Information Resources Access and Client Services areas. In this structure the mould was broken and programmes were redefined from the ground up.

The Australian National University structure is in many ways similar to that at the University of Melbourne. The Division of Information, headed by the Pro Vice-Chancellor, comprises seven main areas (Corporate Information Services; Scholarly Information Services (Library); Scholarly Technology Services; Networks and Communications; Systems and Desktop Services; ANU Supercomputer Facility; and ANU Archives). A recent development has been the move to a programme structure underlying these organizational areas. The 13 programmes focus on enterprise solutions, web solutions, library user services, scholarly information resource management, information literacy, teaching and learning, digital resource management, networks and communications, servers and desktops, ANU supercomputer facility, ANU archives, space management and administration services.

Two other models, at Griffith University and the Queensland University of Technology (QUT), both of which introduced converged structures in the mid-1990s, demonstrate the diversity of approaches adopted. At Griffith, the Division of Information Services, under the leadership of the Pro Vice-Chancellor (Information Services), provides a range of services and products through four service groups (Flexible Learning and Access Services; Information and Communication Technology Services; Learning Services; and Library and Learning Environment Services). The work of these service groups is supported by two further groups, Corporate Services, and Planning and Development Services. At QUT, the Division of Technology, Information and Learning Support includes the areas or departments that provide central support for the academic functions of the faculties and technological support for communication and administration across the institution. Headed by the Deputy Vice-Chancellor (Technology, Information and Learning Support), the Division comprises Information Technology Services, Library Services, Teaching and Learning Support Services, and QUT Printing Services.

Evolution

Although there was a concerted move to implement converged structures in the mid to late 1990s, the subsequent history of convergence in Australia has been one of ebb and flow. Some of the pioneers reverted to more traditional structures within a few years. The University of Tasmania, for example, discontinued its experiment in convergence under which the Library and Information Technology Services were grouped together under a pro-vice-chancellor as Information Services in early 1999, less than five years after its first introduction. As has occasionally happened elsewhere, the dissolution of the Information Services Division followed the departure of the Vice-Chancellor who had been instrumental in its initial formation. And it was probably not coincidental that following the appointment of that same Vice-Chancellor to the University of Melbourne, a converged structure was introduced there. A similar process of dissolution occurred at the University of New South Wales where following changes in personnel the Information Services grouping was discontinued and the Library and Information Technology Services went their separate ways, with the Library currently reporting to the Pro Vice-Chancellor (Education and Quality Improvement) and Information Technology Services to the Deputy Vice-Chancellor (Resources). More recently, in late 2003, a long-standing experiment in convergence, at the University of Canberra, ended. Originally introduced in the early 1990s as an Information Services Division, comprising Information Technology Services, the Library, Printery, Mailroom and Registry, the model was subsequently transformed into a Client Services Division (retaining ITS and the Library, adding Health and Counselling Services but excluding the Printery, Mailroom and Registry). On the dissolution of the Client Services Division, Information Technology Services transferred into the portfolio of the Pro Vice-Chancellor (Research and Information Management), the Library into the portfolio of the Pro Vice-Chancellor (Academic), and Health and Counselling Services into a Corporate Services Division. As the University of Canberra example illustrates, sometimes the grouping of units was driven by a determination not simply to achieve coherence in terms of a developing information infrastructure but also to bring together a much broader range of client-focused services.

Elsewhere converged structures of one kind or other have survived but have changed in terms of their component parts. At the University of the Sunshine Coast the original converged model included Information Technology Services, the Library, Records and Registry, and Reprographics. In July 2003 Information Technology Services was reconstituted as a separate department but the other areas have remained together within an Information Services Division. And at the University of Ballarat the recent transfer of the Learning and Teaching Support group into the School of Education and TAFE Programs has led to the partial disbanding of a formerly comprehensive converged structure previously known as Academic Support Services. The remaining component units (Information and Communications Technologies, the Library, Media Technology and Print Services) have reformed within a new group, Information Services.

The University of Ballarat example is unusual in the light of current trends. A noticeable feature of new or reconfigured convergence models in Australia has been the introduction of a third major partner, the online learning or flexible education centre. Indeed, in some cases, the current converged model comprises just library and online learning services. The name given to such structures reflects their particular focus, for example, Education Services at the University of Newcastle and Learning Services at Deakin University.

Collaboration

As has already been noted, some institutions have adopted what might be termed a relationship model to capture the potential synergies arising out of the growing convergence in function across library and information services. Under this model an emphasis is placed on encouraging collaboration between existing organizational units rather than reforming those units within a new organizational structure. Such an approach avoids both the challenges inherent in bringing together groups of staff with quite different cultures and the taint of ideology if not zealotry that is seen by some to characterize the structural convergence movement.

It is an approach favoured by many Australian universities, including such research-intensive institutions as Monash University, the University of Adelaide, the University of New South Wales, the University of Queensland, the University of Sydney and the University of Western Australia. The award-winning library at the University of Queensland, relabelled in its digital manifestation as the Cybrary, is often cited as evidence of the success of this model. And at the University of Tasmania the dissolution of a converged Information Services structure did not prevent the three separate units, the Library, Information Technology Resources and the Flexible Education Centre, from subsequently working together to introduce a single tiered service or help desk to support their several services. The advocates of this approach would argue that the enabling of convergence in service provision, including, for example, the creation of rich e-learning environments and the development of responsive corporate information systems, does not require integrated organizational structures. They might further suggest that no one model suits every institution and that the ultimate test is one of fitness for purpose. They would probably also concede, however, that the adoption of the relationship or collaborative model assumes the continuing maintenance of good working relationships between the various organizational units at all levels, the sharing of a common vision or purpose, and a strong emphasis on effective communication.

In most reorganizations the prevailing institutional culture plays an important role. Some of the newer and smaller universities seem to be able to adapt to changing needs as they occur whereas such flexibility often proves more difficult in larger and older institutions. It is also true that structural change, at least in the Australian higher education sector, has often been driven by strong personalities and power plays during a time of constant change in which responsibilities have been reviewed and redefined to meet new challenges.

Arguments for and against

The cases for and against the convergence and relationship models, in the context of the Australian experience, may be summarized as follows.

The advantages of the converged or joined-up (marriage vows) approach include:

- the development of a broader knowledge base beyond traditional boundaries enabling new thinking and new roles to emerge
- greater opportunities for collaboration within and outside the group
- better use and development of knowledge and expertise
- greater innovation based on different perspectives and different professional approaches
- an enhanced ability to think critically about information as a strategic resource and hence a capacity to evaluate, rationalize and use information more effectively and efficiently
- better use of infrastructure to optimize business solutions
- the placing of corporate goals ahead of departmental agendas
- the enabling of joined-up thinking, planning and doing
- an ability to set priorities across structures and move resources to achieve them
- an ability to achieve sustainable change through breaking the mould
- an opportunity to transform existing cultures.

Possible disadvantages may be:

- a loss of momentum and of leading-edge advantage as the organization focuses its energy on structural outcomes and personal issues during an initial period of uncertainty
- a requirement for different and often scarce skills such as expertise in mentoring and co-ordinating rather than presiding, defining and organizing.

The advantages of the collaborative or agreed relationship (handshake) model include:

- greater motivation towards individual achievement within the separate parts

- less churn and disruption allowing uninterrupted development and workflow
- an emphasis on the critical need to build relationships
- greater individual responsibility for action rather than the more diffuse responsibility of a larger group.

Possible disadvantages may be:

- a dependence on the expertise and personality of a small number of key managers
- the continuance of role overlap, duplication of function, and diffused responsibility for service provision
- less opportunity for innovation where individuals with different professional skills may contribute to outcomes outside traditional frameworks.

Conclusion

The higher education environment in common with other sectors is undergoing significant change within the global knowledge-based economy. Education has become available anytime/anywhere and competition among providers, especially in the higher education sector, is increasing. The pressure to make better use of knowledge and information to gain strategic advantage is influencing how universities decide to build and develop their information infrastructure.

The investment that universities already make in information management and knowledge creation for competitive advantage is substantial and there is a growing recognition of the need to manage this investment effectively. Inefficient management and use of information and knowledge, lack of alignment to corporate goals, and concerns expressed by stakeholders have led to the development of information structures where responsibilities for university-wide information goals are more clearly defined and where effectiveness and efficiency are key drivers. Collaboration, co-operation and partnership are needed to ensure that a holistic approach is taken to information and knowledge sharing in direct support of the vision and mission of the university. The strategies and operational programmes that achieve the vision are based on function rather than service area and require partnerships across the breadth of the institution. Increasingly universities will focus on the wider information and knowledge environment where open discussion, the sharing of expertise, and addressing knowledge and information gaps become part of their normal business. Greater convergence of information services will ensure that an institution-wide approach to information management enables seamless interactions, which recognize the interdependencies of key suppliers of information resources. In Australia, as elsewhere, the challenge will be to achieve this goal without loss of momentum and credibility in a context where vision and agreed strategic priorities drive structural realignment or, at the very least, a reorientation of services.

References

Australian National University, Information Policy Working Party (1999) *Towards a Competitive Information Environment: planning for the future: report of the Information Policy Working Party*, Canberra, Australian National University.

O'Brien, L. and Sidorko, P. (2000) Integrating Information, Education and Technology Services, *Educause Annual Conference, Nashville, TN*.

20

Convergence in Europe outside the United Kingdom

Mel Collier

Introduction

Convergence of libraries with computing, learning development and other services in universities has been developing since the late 1980s. Early examples were in the USA and the UK, but convergence has progressed most markedly in the UK, where as a proportion of the total number of institutions, there are now many instances of convergence in one form or another, as this volume demonstrates. The trend has also been noticeable in Australia and New Zealand. It appears, however, that in Europe outside the UK convergence is a much rarer phenomenon, of which this contribution offers a preliminary study.

In an earlier study in 1996 (Collier, 1996) the present author analysed the history, development and rationale behind convergence as they appeared mainly in UK at the time. Several themes were identified to which the early trends towards convergence could be attributed, as follows:

- *technocratic imperative* – the notion that information technologies, educational technologies and information services were becoming so intertwined that the relevant skills should be harnessed together
- *executive thrust* – the argument that the strategic and economic implications of IT, information and media services for the success of universities were so great that integrated management and authority should be established
- *information management* – the reasoning that a university as a creator and consumer of information needs to manage three types of information extremely effectively: the universe of recorded knowledge, its own generated research output, and its corporate intelligence

- *resource management* – the argument that academic services consume a great deal of resource and if not converged are inevitably in competition for resources, and that convergence should be able to offer economies
- *electronic scholar* – a user-focused argument (in contrast to the above management-orientated arguments), which characterized the scholar as information navigator roaming the global networks and for whom a totally new type of user service would need to be developed. Given that the concept of the electronic scholar is now universally accepted, we now propose to use the term *user focus*.

By 1996 an additional factor was emerging (which was seemingly not envisaged by the front-runners of the late 1980s), that developments in e-learning would lead to further integration of information services with courseware development and learning environment activities and hence to convergence of those operational functions. Let us call this the *learning environment* argument.

The conclusions of the time were that after ten years the field of convergence in the UK was highly active but still in a state of flux (reflecting the state of flux and change in UK higher education as a whole) and that it was still too early for a coherent theory of convergence management to have emerged. Nearly ten years further on there is now a wealth of experience of converged service management. Elsewhere in Europe (apart from Ireland) the phenomenon of convergence seemed to be unknown in 1996 and when mentioned evoked genuine surprise. It is timely now, therefore, not only to review the state of convergence in UK universities, as in other studies in this book, but in this contribution to assess whether convergence has had any impact in the rest of Europe in the intervening years.

Work since 1996

The work mentioned above (Collier, 1996) contains what is believed to be a full bibliography of the relevant literature up to 1996, which need not be cited again here. Since that time a further body of work has appeared. Convergence was the subject of several works by Pugh, including a British Library Research and Information report and an evaluation of the convergence process at the University of Birmingham. In a review article (Pugh, 2002) he commented on experiences in the UK, primarily from a management theory standpoint, suggesting that convergence is essentially about collaboration, irrespective of management structures, a view with which many concur. However, he also seems to suggest that because administration of information services through the 1990s continued to be enshrined in hierarchic structures, it remained immune from the management theories developing outside libraries, a statement which those managers who engaged in the intense debates and changes of that period would find hard to accept.

In Australia, the Council of Australian University Librarians made a survey of the state of affairs in convergence in 1997 (CAUL, 1997). At that time libraries were part of a wider administrative organization within institutions in 18 cases, as against 13 where they were not. The results shed interesting light on the nature of the convergences, services offered, benefits and pitfalls and future intentions or forecasts.

In the USA there appears to have been something of a resurgence in interest in convergence in recent years, probably due to the pressure to demonstrate student (customer) focus in what we call the *learning environment* argument. For example, integrated student support services have been introduced at Loyola University, where student satisfaction and retention have been key factors. (Orgeron, 2001). Twenty-five liberal arts institutions have formed a group of convergence managers (chief information officers) within the Council on Library and Information Resources (Ferguson, Spencer and Metz, 2004) and there is a library–IT partnerships constituent group and website within Educause (Educause, 2005). It is noticeable that these sources tend to make little or no reference to convergence and the experience thereof outside the USA, even though arguably the more innovative developments have occurred elsewhere.

Returning to the UK it can safely be said that as a proportion of the total number of higher education institutions, the last 15 years has resulted in a greater level of pervasiveness of convergence than in any other country, with the possible exception of Australia. The Society of College, National and University Libraries (SCONUL) carried out an informal survey in 1997, which is no longer available, but each institution is asked a question about convergence in the annual statistical return. The extent of convergence activity is well covered and analysed by Field (Field, 2001) whose bibliography can be regarded as definitive at the date of publication, to which only a few references can now be added.

The approach to reviewing convergence in Europe outside the United Kingdom

As soon as the author was asked to write this contribution it was evident that collecting information on convergence in Europe would not be easy. From the author's extensive experience of working in Europe, both in director positions and also in European projects over the last decade, it was suspected from anecdote, or rather lack of it, that examples of convergence would be few and far between. At the outset only four examples were known, of which two had already de-converged. Furthermore there is no overarching organization in Europe where such intelligence would naturally emerge, as it would through, say SCONUL or the Joint Information Services Committee of the Higher Education Funding Councils (JISC) in the UK or Educause in the USA.

The first step was therefore to use the author's e-mail contacts throughout Europe to announce the study and request information on convergence or at least pointers to information or further contacts. This resulted in some possible participants in the study. When contributors were positively identified they were asked to name any other possible participants, particularly in their country, on the presumption that other examples of convergence would be known to them. The second step was to send the same e-mail message to contacts representing the national library associations in Europe as listed on the International Federation of Library Associations (IFLA, 2005) website. This resulted in only a slight response.

The third step was to carry out a conventional literature search on the relevant abstracting and indexing services. It should be noted here that terminology in this field is by no means standardized. Although the term 'convergence' in the context of co-operation or merger between library and other academic services is generally understood in the UK, it is not so elsewhere. The terms 'integration', 'collaboration' and 'co-operation' must also be submitted as well. Similarly the submitted terms must also embrace 'computing service', 'computing centre', 'IT service', 'ICT service', 'academic service' and so on. The searches were submitted in English, while recognizing the danger of missing references in other languages. As might be expected, searches using these terms resulted in many false drops. The results of this search were also slight. Finally an internet search was carried out following certain lines of enquiry looking for website and other informally published material. Again the results were modest. The results of all these enquiries, which took place between July and September 2004, were as follows.

Institutions where converged services are in operation or services are in process of convergence:

Finland	Kuopion Yliopisto (University of Kuopio)
	Tampereen Teknillinen Yliopisto (Tampere University of Technology)
Germany	Universität Bielefeld
	Brandenburgische Technische Universität Cottbus
	Technische Universität München
	Carl von Ossietzky Universität Oldenburg
	Universität Ulm
	Fachhochschule Zittau/Görlitz

Iceland	Kennaraháskóli Islands (Iceland University of Education)
Netherlands	Universiteit Twente
	Avans Hogeschool (Avans Polytechnic)
	Universiteit van Tilburg
Norway	Norges Landbrukshøgskole (Agricultural University of Norway)
Spain	Universitat Pompeu Fabra
Sweden	Malmö Högskola (Malmö University)
Switzerland	Université de Genève

Institutions where convergence is planned:

Croatia	University J.J. Strossmayer, Osijek
Finland	Lapin Yliopisto (University of Lapland)
	Lappeenrannan Teknillinen Yliopisto (Lappeenranta University of Technology)

Institutions where de-convergence has taken place:

Ireland	Limerick University
Netherlands	University of Amsterdam
Norway	Norges Idretthøgskole (University of Sport and Physical Education)
	A paper on the convergence was published in the official Norwegian science library journal (Vibe, 1998)

Countries where convergence has definitely not occurred at all, according to respondents:

Belgium
France
Hungary
Italy

The questionnaire

When institutions had been positively identified as being involved in convergence, a short questionnaire was sent to the relevant contact. The questionnaire was designed to elicit the key strategic factors in convergence, without going into too much detail, which could be both difficult to compare or integrate and perhaps might also discourage a reply. In this respect, the questionnaire was more concise than the Australian survey (CAUL, 1997). For the avoidance of doubt it was stated in a covering message that by convergence was meant 'the bringing together of library and computing services, and in some cases educational development and learning technology services, under single management'. Where possible the questions were designed to be open in order to allow the respondent to give as much background information as he or she thought appropriate. The questionnaire was piloted first at the University of Twente and the University of Geneva (Genève), after which very minor modifications were made. Eventually ten completed questionnaires were received. The questions are shown below. Analysis of the completed questionnaires follows in the next section.

1 What services are converged and when did this happen?
2 Describe the circumstances and reasons behind the convergence, including who was/were the main instigator(s).
3 Describe briefly the converged organization, management and reporting structure.
4 Was the decision to converge influenced by experience elsewhere? If so please give details.
5 Describe the advantages that have been gained e.g. better customer service, co-operation, economy and efficiency, flexibility, multi-skilling.
6 Describe any disadvantages e.g. poorer service, conflicts.
7 Have there been wider impacts in the institution e.g. major strategic changes, effects on learning or research?
8 Have new types of jobs and services appeared as a result of convergence?
9 What staff development and training programmes have been introduced to support convergence?
10 Has there been any evaluation or customer feedback of the converged organization? If so please give details.
11 Convergence is less common in continental Europe than in UK. Can you suggest why?
12 Are there any internal documents in electronic form that will provide further background and information and that you can provide? If so, please send them.
13 Are there any publicly available documents (formally published or available on the web) that provide additional background or information? If so, please supply references.
14 Please add any further information that you feel to be relevant.

Analysis of responses to the questionnaire by institution

Table 20.1 Analysis of responses to the questionnaire by institution

Institution	Converged services	Since
Kuopio	Library, IT Centre, Photographic Centre, Learning Centre form Information Services.	1999
Bielefeld	In process: proposals include Library IT and Administrative IT to move to Computing Centre. Media Centre to transfer content activities to Library. Computer Centre to run e-learning platform, content administered by Library.	Proposal 2005
Cottbus	Library, Computer Centre, Administrative Computing, Multi-media Centre.	2004
Oldenburg	Library, Computing Centre, Administrative Computing, Media Centre, University Press, Printing Office, University Archive.	2004
	To follow: web master, web content management system, e-learning support and learning management system.	2005–6
Ulm	KIZ (Kommunikations- und Informationszentrum) formed from the Library, Computing Services and Centre for Photography and Reproduction.	2002
Kennaraháskóli Islands	Libraries (4), Media Centre, Teachers' Centre, Computer Department.	2000 2002
Twente	Library, Educational Development, University Press, formed DINKEL. IT Services included, University Press abolished, forming ITBE (IT, Library and Education).	1999 2003
Norges Idretthøgskole	Library, Computing Services.	1998 Ended 1999
Pompeu Fabra	Library, Computing Services, Media.	2003
Genève	Co-ordination of Library Services (libraries belong to faculties) with several central services including Administrative Computing. Formal attachment to IT Division.	1997 1984

Institution	Circumstances, reasoning and instigators
Kuopio	Directors of Library and IT Centre jointly proposed a Learning Centre, which hired pedagogical staff and ICT staff. Co-operation strongly supported by Rector. Role of Information Services is: joint help desk, quality control, joint budget, elimination of overlap, staff flexibility.
Bielefeld	An IT Manager was appointed in 2001 to promote collaboration on ICT University-wide. Grant from the Deutsche Forschungsgemeinschaft (DFG) was catalyst for further restructuring. Proposals prepared by IT Manager, Librarian and Pro-Rector Organizational Development.
Cottbus	Instigated by Executive Board of the University for reasons of efficiency, management flexibility, more synergy and innovation. Plan for a new building led to model of integration. Development of e-learning and DFG funding also factors.
Oldenburg	A steering group was formed to co-ordinate activities and units. Concluded that co-operation between separate units has limits in implementing user-friendly services. Director of Library and Information System and President proposed bid to DFG to support further convergence.
Ulm	Origins go back to 1987 when Prof. Grossmann proposed a converged structure in a government committee, but not realized until 13 years later. Main reason is to support teaching staff in professional use of media and ICT, to improve learning products and facilitate e-material production. Also KIZ aims to create unified infrastructure for the traditional and the e-campus. The latter integrates administration, enrolment, exams management and so on with information management.
Kennarahásköli Islands	Distance education on the internet has been developing since 1993. In 1995 a working group reviewed accommodation for services and proposed to strengthen the computer and network structure. The merger of four institutions in 1998 to form the University, and a new Rector in 2000, gave the opportunity to converge small service divisions under one Director. After visit to England to look at possible models it was decided to develop the new service complex as a learning centre.
Twente	Much study and consultancy preceded convergence. The main instigator was the Rector and convergence was supported by the Library. The 1999 convergence was driven by cross-discipline in teaching and learning, blurring of boundaries by ICT and the need for innovation and entrepreneurship in ICT. In the 2003 process, economy and efficiency played a more prominent role.

Continued on next page

Institution	Circumstances, reasoning and instigators
Norges Idretthøgskole	Weaknesses in computing services were seen as holding back development of digital services for the University. External consultants in 1997 recommended merger with Library. The University Director was the main instigator.
Pompeu Fabra	The Executive Board of the University instigated some administrative and organizational changes. One was the creation of a new area, Information Resources, where Computing Services and Library were merged, for reasons of flexibility, efficiency and innovation.
Genève	A restructuring of Central Administration resulted in the attachment of the Library Co-ordination Service (SEBIB) to the IT Division. Based on positive experiences of the informatics staff, the Chief of SEBIB developed a new vision in support of the move. The Director General of Central Administration proposed and implemented.

Institution	Organization and structure	Influences from elsewhere
Kuopio	Each Centre has a director, one of which is also Director of Information Services, which has an Executive Group and a board of customers. In Autumn 2004 the University decided to complete the unification into one department (one budget, one Director).	Learning resource centres in England.
Bielefeld	Dual Chief Information Officers (CIOs) (IT and Scholarly Information) work closely together in a new IKM strategy group, which includes a Pro-Rector and the Kanzler (University President). There will be a new IT forum representing faculties and services.	
Cottbus	The IKMZ (Informations-, Kommunikations- und Mediazentrum) comprises departments of Network and Security, Computing and Systems, Content and Data Management, Library, Management Information. Each has a head reporting to the CIO, who reports to the Executive Board and has an advisory board.	Twente, Nottingham, Sheffield Hallam, Virginia Tech.

Continued on next page

Institution	Organization and structure	Influences from elsewhere
Oldenburg	Proposal: central unit for integrated information management comprises Library, IT Services and User Services with a management board of four persons, one of whom is CEO reporting to the University President.	UK, USA, Australia. Visited Birmingham, Nottingham, Sheffield Hallam. Goals similar to Nottingham.
Ulm	The formerly autonomous services have not just been brought under one roof, but reorganized into five fully converged departments, comprising Information Systems (includes information services), Infrastructure (network and hardware), Literature Support (bibliography and so on), Literature Administration (acquisitions and so on) and Media. Leadership is under review but will have a strong CEO with HQ staff.	Ulm is the first university in Germany to realize convergence so other examples at the time were not available. It is thought that international research was not carried out.
Kennaraháskóli Islands	There is a strategic management team comprising the Director, Head of Library and Head of Computer and Media Centre. The Heads report to the Director, who reports to the Rector.	Sheffield Hallam, Malmö.
Twente	ITBE has matrix structure of expertise and product groups. Groups have heads who are members of the management team, which reports to the Managing Director of ITBE who reports to the University Board. Faculty committees participate in policy development.	Experiences elsewhere were studied in the work of the consultants and preparatory committees.
Norges Idretthøgskole	Converged organization headed by Chief Librarian. Computing Services section leader reported to Chief Librarian, who reported to University Director.	No influence from elsewhere.
Pompeu Fabra	Information Resources has a Head (the former Library Director) and the Library, and Computing Services with Media both have a Director. These three, with the section heads, form the management team.	

Continued on next page

Institution	Organization and structure	Influences from elsewhere
Genève	All administrative and technical services are attached to the Central Administration. The Head of SEBIB reports to the Head of the IT Division. SEBIB manages the library system for all libraries in Genève.	A joint team of IT and library specialists was formed in the 1970s for library automation. This was a natural progression.

Institution	Advantages gained	Disadvantages, problems
Kuopio	Information reaches customers better. Staff more customer orientated. Joint quality control. Cross boundary working, flexibility of staff. Joint budget gives more flexibility.	Implementation takes much time and management effort. Most staff positive but a few not.
Bielefeld	In process – too early to say	
Cottbus	Still early but new building will offer better customer service. More efficiency and multi-skilling expected in longer term. Focus should not be on short term saving of money.	Fears of change and loss of unit identity. New structure is radical – may not be understood. Standardization may be seen as reduction of the individual or faculty-related service.
Oldenburg	Coherent planning of identity management system, portal solutions, IT and information literacy programmes, web based exam administration, e-learning strategy. Flexibility of resources, better mutual understanding. Multi-skilling and economies will follow.	Implementation is time-consuming. Many staff fearful of change.
Ulm	Better customer service, co-operation, flexibility and multi-skilling. More efficient structure has brought savings, which enabled a new media compartment to be created without increased spending. A common customer-friendly front office.	Wide ranging changes led to difficulties: some people did not want to change, some had to move and work for new superiors.

Continued on next page

Institution	Advantages gained	Disadvantages, problems
		Management is aware of need for culture change and will introduce staff development.
Kennaraháskóli Islands	Management according to shared vision. Better co-operation but still room for more flexibility. New Learning Centre helped create positive attitude by teachers from former different schools, and team working by LC staff.	At first temporary conflicts between staff groups, but this has eased with time. We have learned to manage change better.
Twente	Cost reductions have been achieved. Innovation in teaching and learning – learning environment, digital library. Co-operation on project proposals and winning external funds.	Two rounds of change in climate of cuts was de-motivating and needs attention. Internal processes, skills and competences need development. Service outputs lower because of reduced faculty budgets. New integrated vision not yet reached.
Norges Idretthøgskole	Better customer service, co-operation, efficiency and flexibility.	No major disadvantages. Earlier frustrations with computing services sometimes reflected on Library.
Pompeu Fabra	Staff more customer orientated and flexible. Better use of resources, customer better service quality. More efficiency and innovation.	No disadvantages, at most minor problems. Implementation takes time and management effort. Staff skills need development.

Continued on next page

Institution	Advantages gained	Disadvantages, problems
Genève	Technological benefits and surer investment-ment choices for libraries. Better awareness of IT people of library needs. Better environment for libraries to launch innovative projects.	Questioning by IT people of bringing librarians into their division. Difficulties in identifying complementarities. Difficulty in keeping attention of IT people after the interesting initial phase of a project. Difficulty in co-ordinating competences and calendars for new projects or changes.

Institution	Wider impacts in the institution
Kuopio	Administrative structure improved in relation to central administration. Teaching and learning services significantly improved. Research services improved. Library services have improved and further integrated with pedagogical and research services.
Bielefeld	In process – too early to say.
Cottbus	We now have one major strategy instead of three or four. This promises avoidance of duplication and promotion of networking. Otherwise too early to say.
Oldenburg	The converged service has supported the change to the BA/MA structure with its new examinations system and course evaluation tool. Previous fragmented infrastructure for e-learning will be co-ordinated by implementing e-learning strategy.
Ulm	The implications of the KIZ concept are currently subject to intense research.
Kennaraháskóli Islands	It is difficult to assess the impact, but it is believed that convergence has had a positive contribution in coping with 60% increase in undergraduates and postgraduates, when staff numbers have remained the same. The environment for distance learning has been strengthened. The new building and technological developments have helped students be more able to use technology.

Continued on next page

Institution	Wider impacts in the institution
Twente	Strategic framework for ITBE is formulated in discussion with faculties and the board. Learning environment improved as a result of higher priority for ICT in teaching and learning.
Norges Idretthøgskole	Convergence lasted too short a time to say.
Pompeu Fabra	Important change in strategic innovation. Significant improvements to teaching and learning expected.
Genève	Better knowledge of technology by the libraries, and faster uptake of new activities. We anticipate impact in the area of e-learning.

Institution	New jobs and services	Staff development and training
Kuopio	The Learning Centre services were all new, with 14 new employees. Student facilities (250 workstations), teachers' facilities, for example pedagogic and IT training.	Everybody gets training programmes, for example quality, customer service, technology. Each unit has own sessions on co-operation.
Bielefeld	Two CIOs (Librarian and IT Manager) More services will be offered as 'one-stop shop'. Library could offer advice on e-learning platform to students and instructors.	
Cottbus	Not yet – only the CIO. More management skills will be needed at higher levels and control and benchmarking will be more important.	Staff members whose jobs will expand get specific training. The main issue is to understand the network that he or she is working within.
Oldenburg	Not yet, expected later.	Programmes to be introduced this year to include qualifications for new or extended services and for key skills and management.
Ulm	The new media service has been introduced with information designers pursuing media-pedagogical and media-psychological approaches.	New programmes will be introduced in 2005.

Continued on next page

Institution	New jobs and services	Staff development and training
Kennaraháskóli Islands	No new jobs specifically but jobs are evolving. New building offers services for conferences which need technical assistance. Rapid increase of distance study makes more demand on services.	Meeting structure ensures staff know what's going on and how to deal with problems. Annual staff development interviews. Funds available to support development.
Twente	No new jobs but tasks have changed. Existing services are constantly renewed. New services such as institutional repository not necessarily due to convergence.	For the 1999 convergence a management development programme was carried through. Not yet for 2003 programme.
Norges Idretthøgskole	Convergence lasted too short a time.	Convergence lasted too short a time.
Pompeu Fabra	Not yet, expected later.	Skills and competence programme for management team. Similar programme expected for all staff.
Genève	No new jobs. A studio for the virtual library is envisaged.	Training sessions for librarians. Three-day seminar for heads. Website on IT division.

Institution	Evaluation or feedback
Kuopio	Customer satisfaction is measured every year. Targeted surveys are carried out and customers are systematically asked to give feedback in training. Self-evaluation is done once per year and there will be an audit in 2005.
Bielefeld	Too early.
Cottbus	There is an advisory council and focus groups for different topics. There will be external evaluation.
Oldenburg	In the first phase there were four focus groups of customers. There will be questionnaires. An advisory council (deans and other stakeholders) will give regular feedback on strategy and services. A group of external experts will evaluate the process of convergence.

Continued on next page

Institution	Evaluation or feedback
Ulm	Empirical research is planned to create a database that will support future staff development.
Kennaraháskóli Islands	Separate surveys for the Library and the Computer and Media Centre.
Twente	There will be an evaluation in the near future.
Norges Idretthøgskole	In 1999 the computing customers section won the 'best service award'. This was won by the Library twice.
Pompeu Fabra	Too early to say.
Genève	This has not been formally evaluated but informally we can say that the libraries are glad to have an intermediary close to the IT people to defend their needs, and anticipate specifications and tools of use to the libraries. On the other hand many believe that the libraries themselves should not be part of IT services.

Discussion

The most immediate observation from this study is that the occurrence of convergence in Europe outside the UK is extremely rare. Some caution in this statement must be expressed owing to the informal nature of the intelligence gathering for this study. Because of the limited time available for the study, information has been collected through a grapevine of contacts, and contacts of contacts. A definitive study would need to be carried out through the good offices of formal associations of librarians, IT managers and educational development people in all of the European countries, which would be a mammoth task. It should also be noted that no serious effort has been made in this study to reach universities in Eastern Europe or Russia. On the other hand it is hard to believe that significant numbers of new examples would be discovered by such a process, given the general effectiveness of the professional grapevine at least in the library world. Our hypothesis must remain that conditions and attitudes among the relevant stakeholders outside the UK may not be conducive to convergence compared with the situation in the UK, the USA, Australia, and New Zealand.

While convergence in those areas has occurred through the individual initiative of institutions (in keeping as it should be with the independence of universities) the existence of vigorous professional associations and (in the UK) the watchful eye of the Higher Education Funding Councils must certainly have been an enabling and encouraging factor. Such encouragement does not generally seem to have been influential at national level in other countries, perhaps with two exceptions.

In Finland there has been an excellent record in recent years of beneficial intervention at national level as, for instance, in the highly successful national digital library (FinELib) programme, which was evaluated in 2002 (Varis and Saari, 2003). Similarly it has been recognized at national level in Finland that information management needs long-term strategic planning at top level in the university and that the traditional independent operation of academic services in universities is no longer appropriate. It has even been observed that 'particular emphasis has been placed on estrangement between the administration and the computer centre in many universities' (Kytömäki, 1995). Further evidence of activity at national level is provided by Haarala (2001).

In Germany there has been the most vigorous intervention of all, where the Deutsche Forschungsgemeinschaft (DFG; German Research Foundation) has made funds available on a competitive basis for proposals for new concepts of co-operation between libraries, computer centres, media centres and faculties. (Deutsche Forschungsgemeinschaft, 2004) From the first round the universities of München and Oldenburg received funding. A second round is in progress.

Some of the respondents to the questionnaire refrained from passing an opinion as to why the situation should be so different from the UK. Some who did suggested that universities in the rest of Europe could be innately more conservative than in Britain, and that faculties usually have much more devolved power (and financial control), which can oppose radical central initiatives. More than one respondent attributed the reason to the Humboldt ideals of the unity of research and teaching and academic freedom, which is to some extent a similar point. It has been pointed out that in Germany, for instance, there are old-fashioned or rigid university statutes that inhibit this sort of change and make it a long, slow process. It is also observed that services may often be headed by academics, sometimes in rotation or by election, which can militate against the development and progression of a professional cadre who would look at developments elsewhere and steer through radical changes. It has also been remarked that in many countries the position of libraries and librarians within the power structure of universities is not strong, which renders the sort of convergence that has occurred in the Anglo-American–Australasian orbit unthinkable. Faculty members in these circumstances can be genuinely amazed by suggestions that librarians should have a role in information strategies, educational development or e-learning. One of the respondents observed that in such circumstances librarians are busy enough developing basic services without getting involved in ambitious enterprises. Another felt that if convergence took place the library would always be the weaker or second class partner in regard to salaries and to competition for resources. Another turned the question round and suggested that the UK has gone further because budgets cuts have forced efficiency and economy measures and the maturity of the university library system allows more innovation.

Regarding the rationale behind convergence the reasons given by respondents are fairly evenly spread between the factors identified in the author's earlier study. *Technocratic imperative* is still strong as are *resource management* and *executive thrust*. *User focus* figures perhaps more strongly than earlier and, as one might expect, the *learning environment* argument is now well to the fore. The German national initiative puts much emphasis on the need for effective *information management* across the university, particularly for research. It should be mentioned at this point that, not referring to any institution in particular, that personalities have often been observed to be a key factor in convergence. While no university would normally admit to making important changes solely on the basis of personalities, it is undoubtedly the case that the presence of managers with the drive and competence to carry through the process can be an influencing factor.

Regarding structures the whole range of approaches observed in earlier studies are represented in the responses, including management under a single executive manager, joint management, rotation of chairmanship and direction by a pro-rector or similar officer. Perhaps the most radical convergence model of those surveyed is that described at Ulm, where five very different units have been created out of the original three, including a completely new unit for media support to teaching and learning (Universität Ulm, 2005). In this respect it could be said to be analogous in the scale and nature of its reorganization to Birmingham (Field, 2001). The Ulm correspondent also observed that in order to realize the full benefits of efficiency and effectiveness the management of a converged service must be granted autonomy over budgets and personnel. The American usage of chief information officer (CIO) is creeping in as a title for the executive manager of the few converged services that exist with at least six occurrences known. This title also occurs where convergence does not exist, for example at the University of Amsterdam where the post-holder has a strategic policy role rather than executive manager role.

Advantages claimed tend to reflect the original rationale for the convergence in each institution: better customer service, better strategic planning, better use of technology, better co-operation and, occasionally, economies. Problems most frequently cited are the time and effort required for convergence and managing the human aspects. It is difficult to identify a trend in wider impact in the institution, given that the response group is small and there has been too little time for impacts to be assessed. Except at Kuopio and Ulm, it is interesting that convergence does not seem to have led to significant numbers of newly defined posts or job descriptions.

This period since 1996 has also seen a few examples of de-convergence. One of the earliest converged services at the University of Limerick in Ireland was de-converged in about 1999. Norges Idretthøgskole experienced a very short-lived convergence. At the University of Amsterdam an attempt was made at convergence, which seems never to have become well established and did not last very long. Among the possible reasons in the latter case are that the roles of the managers involved may not have been properly defined and agreed. Currently the problem of co-ordinating information and IT in what is a very large and complex University has been approached by the appointment of a non-executive CIO, as mentioned above.

Conclusions

The initial impression that convergence in Europe outside the UK is rare is obviously supported by this study. In fact, so few examples have been found in relation to the number of institutions that convergence could be considered to be a negligible feature in information services development in European higher education as a whole, outside the UK. Our hypothesis is that conditions in Europe are generally not conducive to convergence. Such conditions could include: powerful decentralized administrations, conservative policies, and the level of maturity or professionalization of university services. That is not to say that where professionalization is strong, convergence would naturally follow. It is evident from experience in the countries where convergence is common, that convergence is not considered the right approach in some or even many institutions.

So far as is known, this contribution is the first attempt to assess the state of affairs with convergence in Europe outside the UK. The fact that the number of known examples is small raises an intriguing question: is convergence still at an early stage in continental Europe and the coming years will see a steady growth as in the Anglo-American–Australasian orbit, or are the conditions fundamentally not conducive and convergence will not develop further? Only further studies in due time will provide the answer.

Acknowledgements

The author wishes to thank the following persons who have either responded to the questionnaire or otherwise provided helpful comments and information:

Aparac-Jelusic, Tatiana	Osijek
Aymonin, David	Lausanne
Baum, Florian	Ulm

Cabo, Mercè	Barcelona
Daalmans, Peter	Twente
Degkwitz, Andreas	Cottbus
Gallart, Nuria	Barcelona
Grossmann, Hans Peter	Ulm
Indriðadottir, Kristín	Reykavík
Løchen, Sølvi	Trondheim
Lossau, Norbert	Bielefeld
Montserrat Espinós	Barcelona
Morriello, Rossana	Venezia
Roten, Gabrielle von	Genève
Simons, Ellen	's-Hertogenbosch
Spangenberg, Marietta	Zittau/Görlitz
Stange, Kari	Stockholm
Stray, Paul	Ås, Norway
Teglási, Ágnes	Budapest
Verhagen, Nol	Amsterdam
Vibe, Anne-Mette	Oslo
Voutilainen, Ulla	Kuopio, now based at Savonia Polytechnic
Wätjen, Hans-Joachim	Oldenburg
Young, Gordon	Limerick

References

Collier, M. (1996) The Context of Convergence. In Oldroyd, M., *Staff Development in Academic Libraries: present practice and future challenges*, London, Library Association Publishing.

Council of Australian University Librarians (1997) *CAUL Questionnaire – Integration of Library and Computer Services*, Lismore, Southern Cross University (SCU), 12 May.

Deutsche Forschungsgemeinschaft (2004) *Leistungszentren für Forschungsinformation – ein Förderinitiative der Deutsche Forschungsgemeinschaft (DFG) zur Stärkung der Informations-Infrastrukturen an deutschen Hochschulen und Förschungseinrichtungen*, Bonn, Germany.

Educause (2005) www.educause.edu.

Ferguson, C., Spencer, G. and Metz, T. (2004) Greater than the Sum of its Parts: the integrated IT/library organization, *Educause Review*, **39** (3), 39–46.

Field, C.D. (2001) Theory and Practice: reflections on convergence in United Kingdom universities, *Liber Quarterly*, **11** (3), 267–89.

Haarala, A.-R. (2001) Libraries as Key Players at Local Level, http://edoc.hu-berlin.de/eunis2001/e/Haarala/HTML/haarala-ch2.html.

IFLA (2005) Membership website, www.ifla.org/database/directy.htm#MD.

Kytömäki, P. (1995) The Future of Libraries and Computer Centres: together or apart? Solutions in Finland, IATUL Conference Enschede, www.iatul.org/conference/proceedings/vol05/papers/Kytomaki.html.

Orgeron, E. (2001) Integrated Academic Student Support Services at Loyola University: the library as a resource clearing house, *Journal of Southern Academic and Special Librarianship*, 2 (3), http://southernlibrarianship.icaap.org/content/v02n03/orgeron_e01.htm.

Pugh, L. (2002) La Convergence en Bibliothèques Universitaires: expériences au Royaume-Uni, *Bulletin des Bibliothèques de France*, 47 (1), 47–59.

Universität Ulm (2005) KIZ website, http://kiz.uni-ulm.de.

Varis, T and Saari, S. (2003) Knowledge Society in Progress – Evaluation of the Finnish Electronic Library – FinElib, Helsinki, Publications of the Finnish Higher Education Council 4.

Vibe, A.-M. (1998) Med Røtter og Vinger?: om sammenslåing av IT og bibliotek, Synopsis 6, www.abm-utvikling.no/publisert/Synopsis/1998/nr-6/syn6-09.htm#TopOfPage.

21

Convergence in the United States

Larry Hardesty

Introduction

To provide a current and comprehensive overview of the relationships between libraries and computer centres among the more than 3000 institutions of higher education in the USA is both daunting and probably impossible. For many institutions, the relationship between the two units is dynamic, with library and computer centres always converging and de-converging. Added to the difficulty of addressing the topic is that it often appears that the converging of academic libraries and computer centres is announced with great fanfare. The president or the newly installed chief academic officer makes the announcement using such words and phrases as 'forward thinking,' 'wave for the future,' and 'essential'. When computer centres and libraries de-converge the institution seldom publicizes this change, and one only learns about them through word of mouth – often at conferences over late night drinks and discussed in hushed tones – 'Did you hear what happened at . . .?' Therefore, relying only on print sources often gives the observer a misleading impression as to the current situation.

Furthermore, the terms 'convergence' and 'de-convergence' can describe a wide range of organizational relationships. In fact, those two terms are not often used in the USA to describe the relationship between librarians and computer centres. More often terms like 'merged' or 'integrated' are used. Whatever term is used (and I will use converged and de-converged in this chapter), the term can describe a variety of situations. 'Convergence' can be used to describe a structure wherein the two organizations report to the same administrator but with little contact between the rank and file further down the organizational chart. It can also be used to describe a structure wherein librarians and computer centre personnel work shoulder to shoulder in the same building (and often at the same desk) with increasingly similar titles, responsibilities and backgrounds. Or, to add to the confusion, it can be used to describe organizations anywhere between these two ends of the spectrum.

Finally, of course, whatever description is used, upon further investigation, it may or may not accurately reflect what is actually being done. As Edward Meachen (2000, 89–90) found, many of the so-called mergers are only 'skin deep' with no thoroughgoing organizational restructuring. Nevertheless, with these caveats, I will plunge ahead.

Background

Discussions of convergence and de-convergence of academic libraries and computer centres are not new in the USA. They have been occurring for more than a full generation. In the early 1980s Patricia Battin (1984) headed at Columbia University probably the first merger between a library and a computer centre. Even earlier Robert Plane (1981), then president of Clarkson College of Technology, wrote about the possible merger of the two units. Many observers in the early 1980s, in fact, predicted the convergence, even the merger of the two units. Such interest existed in the topic at that time that Richard Dougherty, then Dean of the libraries at the University of Michigan, founded a publication, *Libraries and Computer Centers: issues of mutual concern*, to explore library and computer centre relations. Nevertheless, after the initial flurry of discussion and debate, by the late 1980s this movement seemed to have lost its momentum.

In 1988, an Association of College and Research Libraries (ACRL) Task Force reported, 'Nearly all of the libraries (90 percent) reported no change in the reporting structure at either director level (computing or library) is under active consideration' (ACRL Task Force, 1988, 4). Dougherty discontinued his publication in 1989, and in the last issue Pat Molholt reported, 'Predicted mergers [of libraries and computer centres] – perhaps never comfortable to either side – has evolved into a kind of functional cooperation' (1989, 286). By 1994, Arthur Young estimated perhaps no more than 25 smaller institutions had brought the library and the computer centre together as a single administrative unit (1994, 5). The merger of the two units, which Molholt described as 'predicted, ballyhooed, and anxiously anticipated' (1989, 1), had been greatly exaggerated – at least in its early years.

Re-emergence

Just when many thought the convergence and de-convergence debate had ended, it re-emerged in the mid-1990s with renewed energy. Why did this happen? Peggy Seiden and Michael Kathman (2000) observed that by the early 1990s information technology permeated the entire higher education market. With this expansion of information technology, the computer centre also became the new 'black hole' down which academic institutions threw more and more money. At the same time, higher education faced increased demands for accountability and fiscal responsibility. Presidents, governing boards and others looked for ways to reduce costs. I am reminded, as one example of evidence of this search to save money, of the response from the chief academic officer at the small private college where I served when I first discussed with him ACRL's *Information Literacy Competency Standards for Higher Education*. I hoped I could interest him in information literacy and could gain his support for library efforts in this direction. Instead, he responded that promoting information literacy would be a good way to make use of the computers on which the institution had spent so much money. No doubt an interest in getting a good return on all the investment in technology has had a considerable impact on the discussion of the relationships between computer centres and libraries in the USA.

Technology alone, however, also has a considerable impact on the relationships of the two units in this country. During the 1990s, library technology moved from the backroom of the academic library to the public services areas. Reference librarians became increasingly technologically skilled, and the responsibilities and skills of librarians and computer centre personnel increasingly overlapped – and appeared even more so to presidents, governing boards, and others who viewed them from a distance. At the same time, desktop computing became available for the faculty and students. They often needed help with their desktop computing and it often did not matter to them from whom it came.

Therefore, one of the first attempts to converge the functions of the two units manifested itself in the idea of combining the computer centre's help desk and the library's reference desk. Students using technology often have reference questions, and students with technology questions often look to whomever convenient to answer them, whether it is someone from the computer centre or a nearby librarian.

Computer centres and library relations among small colleges

Anticipating the continued discussion of convergence and the increased interest among library directors at small colleges in the topic prompted me to conduct in the mid-1990s a study of the changing roles and relationships between the two units. With the financial support of the Council on Library and Information Resources, I interviewed 40 computer centre administrators and 51 librarians (49 library directors) at 51 small colleges throughout the USA between January 1994 and October 1996. Most of the institutions at which I interviewed individuals belonged to the Oberlin Group, a loosely structured organization of 74 of the financially stronger private liberal arts colleges in the USA. Subsequently, I reported the results in several publications (Hardesty, 1997a, 1997b, 1998, 2000), including the book I edited, *Books, Bytes, and Bridges* (2000).

Essentially, I found in the mid-1990s that most computer centres and libraries at small colleges had neither merged nor closely converged. Few small colleges had chief information officer positions (CIOs) with responsibilities for both the computer centre and the library. In addition, I concluded few of the directors of either unit supported the concept of a merged organizational structure or the CIO position, and even fewer at the time thought a merged organization structure or a CIO position a good idea for their own institution.

Currently, about 20% of these Oberlin Group institutions have some form of a converged structure, although far fewer have anything resembling a completely converged structure. In recent years overall there has been a slight increase in the number of institutions within the group where some element of the computer operations reported to the library directors. There have also been a few institutions that have de-converged, most notably Gettysburg College (Wagner, 2000). Overwhelmingly among the Oberlin Group, when both units report to the same individual, they report to the library director. In a few cases, the library director has moved to the position of CIO and another individual is employed with the title of library director or a comparable title.

Who heads a converged organization?

Why has the library director most frequently become the CIO at these small institutions? Each situation has its unique characteristics, but I suspect most library directors, at this time, tend to have more managerial skills than most computer centre directors. As an organizational unit, libraries have a long history with established functions. Frequently, I found, the computer centre directors at these small institutions started as faculty members with an interest in technology or as data processing personnel in the business office. Ten or 15 years later they found themselves managing complex organizations with a very diverse staff and a seemingly insatiable appetite for resources.

Librarians, while we may complain about our lack of preparation for our profession, generally in the USA have the minimum degree of the Masters in

Library Science, or, more recently, a Masters in Library and Information Science. It provides a common experience, socialization to the profession and perhaps indoctrination to certain service values.

Computer centre personnel, while no less talented and capable, do not have this common experience. They frequently come to academic institutions from business and industry and the military, and often without an advanced degree, and, occasionally, even without an undergraduate degree. While there is diversity in values, attitudes and experiences among librarians, particularly between those in public and technical services, this diversity often pales in comparison with the diversity one often finds in computer services personnel. A computer centre often has a much a more diverse staff than the library, and it often does not have the long history within an organization that the library usually has.

Therefore, we should not be surprised when computer centres provided particularly challenging units as their responsibilities, staff and budget continued to grow by leaps and bounds. We also should not be surprised when administrators and governing boards looked at a seemingly similar, but historically more stable, organization – the library – for assistance in managing this new organization, which seemed to consume resources without either an end in sight or a clear return on investment.

Meachen (2000) reached a similar conclusion in his study of the computing and library relations in the University of Wisconsin System. This is a large state university system with two doctoral granting institutions, 11 comprehensive institutions, 13 two-year colleges and an independent extension service. While I had largely interviewed first generation computer centre directors and CIOs among the private liberal colleges, Meachen examined these organizations as they come to maturation and begin looking for second generation CIOs outside the organization. He found that higher administrators viewed library directors as effective managers and knowledgeable about technology. Also important, they saw library directors as working more closely with the faculty and academic administrators and having more credibility with the faculty than did computing professionals. He wrote, 'In every case involving internal promotion in the University of Wisconsin system, the manager chosen was the librarian, not the computer services director' (Meachen, 2000, 91). As the computer centre matures as an organization and information technology matures as a profession, this situation probably will change. As one computer centre director (a sociologist by education) told me, 'It is not that we are not professionals, but we are not yet a profession.'

Advantages of closer convergences and mergers

Despite my personal scepticism about some of the rhetoric used to justify closer convergences and mergers, there are advantages of closer convergences, and perhaps even mergers, between computer centres and libraries. Raymond Neff (2000) reflected in his essay on reasons for considering a merger and a separation. Essentially, he wrote, nearly every institution of higher education has embraced information technology, and libraries have become increasingly dependent on it. Networking has allowed consortial searching of both library and computer resources on a level only imaged just a few years ago. Whether or not this leads to a merger of the two units (not just them closely working together) depends on many local factors.

Among the advantages proposed in the literature in the USA include:

1   Users are often unable to distinguish between responsibilities of computer centres and libraries and are confused about who to ask for assistance (Ferguson, Spencer and Metz, 2004). Better service can be provided to users through a merged organization (Engeldinger, 2000; Dowell and White, 2000).
2   The units have overlapping missions, structures, constituents and budgets. Mergers can increase synergies and flexibility and reduce competition for resources (Ferguson, Spencer and Metz, 2004).
3   The role of the staff is enhanced. The head of the merged unit is more likely to serve as the higher administrative level than either the heads of unmerged units and is in more of a position to see the bigger picture of the institution's mission and goals (Meachen, 2000). Professional staffs assume more technical, managerial, and instructional responsibilities (Engeldinger, 2000).
4   Merged units aid in recruitment of new staff members (Dowell and White, 2000).

Disadvantages of closer convergences and mergers

Obviously there are some disadvantages – or else all the computer centres and academic libraries would have merged by now. Inertia alone cannot explain why most have not.

Among the disadvantages proposed in the literature in the USA are:

1   Librarians and computer centre personnel come from different cultures and bringing them closely together can create more problems than they solve (Hardesty, 2000, 74). Some observers consider this an overplayed reason for opposing mergers (Engeldinger, 2000, 115) and point out the differences

within libraries. I would argue there are some general differences, as I have argued elsewhere (Hardesty, 2000, 74–7), but they are not insurmountable. Obviously, some institutions appeared to have overcome any differences. Still, I would also argue that without careful attention to the difference that can occur, serious problems can arise, as described by Robin Wagner (2000) in her essay 'The Gettysburg Experience'. As one unnamed computer centre director told me, 'You can make all the beautiful speeches you want, but it will take a lot to make it successful.'

2   Whomever is chosen to lead the merged unit (library director or computer centre director) they are probably unprepared by education or experience to lead the other unit (Meachen, 2000, 93). In my experience as an academic library director, it would appear difficult for a library director to assume responsibility for a complex unit for which he or she does not have years of experience without 1) neglecting the library and 2) feeling unprepared to direct the other unit. I think the same observation would be accurate for computer centre directors. Placing the head of one unit in charge of both can result in that person being viewed as an interloper in one location and as negligent in fulfilling previously held responsibilities in the other.

3   Mergers save neither personnel nor money. While some claim savings through closer convergence (Oke, 2003), the argument is not compelling, or, as a minimum not sufficiently so to generalize very far about it. In fact, even those who support closer integration are quick to point out, 'Merging primarily to save money or reduce staffing will present significant obstacles to success. These motivating factors almost always lead to a downward spiral in service quality and staff morale – a situation that quickly becomes debilitating' (Ferguson, Spencer and Metz, 2004, 2).

4   Mutual goals can be accomplished without the risks and uncertainly of more closely converging the two units. Frequently individuals I interviewed referred to joint ventures, such as newsletters, regularly scheduled meals and meetings together, and other efforts to establish and maintain good communications between the two units. Often at small colleges the good relationships between the two units are based on personal friendships (Hardesty, 2000). Separate units can collaborate and work together for mutual goals, and merged units do not necessarily mean everyone will work together in harmony.

The future

Where are computer centre and academic library relationships in the USA headed? As the American baseball player, Yogi Berra, once reportedly said, 'It is hard to make predictions, particularly about the future.' I think it relatively easy to predict that academic libraries will increasingly become users of computer technology, as will almost every other unit on campus, whether it is the registrar's office, the business office or the classroom. Like the small child who, when given a hammer, suddenly discovers everything needs to be hammered (and some things do), we are still in a phase in which it sometimes appears that everything would benefit from a good application of technology. We are still discovering where technology enhances what we wish to accomplish and where it does not. For example, not so long ago many observed we would all be working from home, but we discovered we are social animals and want to interact with each other – at least some of the time. I suspect we have similar lessons to learn about distance education – and computer centre and library relations.

No doubt we will see continued and enhanced collaboration and co-operation between computer centres and academic libraries. There are many successful examples in *Books, Bytes and Bridges* (Hardesty, 2000). While this will bring computer centres and academic libraries closer together, I see no technological imperative or manifest destiny in them becoming single units. At some institutions it will happen and at some it will not. Why? Probably there are three answers: personality, personality and personality.

The answer, of course, is a bit more complex than this but not much. I speculate those who support close convergence are more risk takers, earlier adopters, feel more comfortable with ambiguity and enjoy working the technology. Those less supportive are more cautious, take more of a wait and see attitude, value tradition, and feel more comfortable managing units in which they have some depth of knowledge. This does not make either type of individual good or bad. Each can value highly the same mission (service to the user) but simply approach achieving it differently. Each personality type has its limitations. The early adopter can just as easily lead a group to a disaster as the resister can keep an important idea or technology from being adopted for the good of the group (Rogers, 1995).

From my study, the need for closer convergence is seldom obvious to the majority of the directors of each unit. Most efforts to bring them together originated from the top down, which, again, does not necessarily make it a bad idea. To many observers, however, the advantages of highly converged organizations are neither readily apparent nor easily achievable. Clifford Lynch, Executive Director of the Coalition of Networked Information, wrote in Arnold Hirshon's *Integrating Computer and Library Services* (1998), 'Merging the functions is an expensive, complex, risky investment under the best of circumstances, and is a terrible way to try to repair an environment in which effective collaboration isn't happening, or to shore up one or more dysfunctional organizational units' (Lynch, 1998, v).

So far the history of converging and de-converging of computer centres and libraries in the USA has not shown us a clear model. Arnold Hirshon found, 'Institutional decisions to integrate or reverse integration and the names of CIOs, change frequently' (1998, 35–7). This suggests we are still looking for the right solutions – to sometimes undefined problems.

I posit that we expect too much from the organizational structure and should look more carefully at the people involved. From my study of the convergence phenomenon it is the people who matter much more than the organizational structure. Close convergence or integration can work, but the more traditional structures also can work. As one library director I interviewed succinctly put it, 'The one thing I discovered is that structure does not mean a tinker's damn. If people have a good attitude and can communicate, structure does not matter.' There is not a single way that works for all institutions. What can be a very productive structure for one organization can be a disaster for another because of the personalities involved. Just as with mathematics, there is no royal road to successful computer centre and academic library relationships, and one size does not fit all – which should keep the convergence and de-convergence discussion going for at least another generation.

References

Association of College and Research Libraries Task Force on Libraries and Computer Centers (1988) *Final Report Chicago*, Chicago, ACRL.

Battin, P. (1984) The Electronic Library: a vision of the future, *Educom Bulletin*, (summer), 12–17, 34.

Dowell, C. and White, A. (2000) Connecticut College: working outside the dictates of the traditional organizational chart. In Hardesty, L. (ed.), *Books, Bytes and Bridges: libraries and computer centers in academic institutions*, Chicago, American Library Association.

Engeldinger, E. (2000) The Service Imperative: a case study for merging libraries and computing centers at smaller academic institutions. In Hardesty L. (ed.), *Books, Bytes and Bridges: libraries and computer centers in academic institutions*, Chicago, American Library Association.

Ferguson, C., Spencer, G. and Metz, T. (2004) Greater Than the Sum of Its Parts: the integrated IT/Library organization, *Educause Review,* (May/June), 38–47.

Hardesty, L. (1997a) Library and Computer Center Relations at Smaller Academic Institutions, *Library Issues*, (September), 1–4.

Hardesty, L. (1997b) Relationships between Libraries and Computer Centers at Liberal Arts Colleges, *Research Briefs*, (November), 1–2.

Hardesty, L. (1998) Computer Center–Library Relations at Smaller Institutions: a look from both sides, *Cause/Effect*, (spring), 35–41.

Hardesty, L. (2000) Computer Center and Library Relations among Small Colleges. In Hardesty L. (ed.), *Books, Bytes and Bridges: libraries and computer centers in academic institutions*, Chicago, American Library Association.

Hirshon, A. (1998) *Integrating Computing and Library Services: an administrative planning implementation guide for information resources*, CAUSE Professional Paper Series 18, Boulder, Colorado, CAUSE.

Information Literacy Competency Standards for Higher Education, American Library Association (2004), www.ala.org/acrl/ilcomstan.html (accessed 1 Aug 2004).

Lynch, C. (1998) Foreword. In Hirshon, A., *Integrating Computing and Library Services: an administrative planning implementation guide for information resources*, CAUSE Professional Paper Series 18, Boulder, Colorado, CAUSE.

Meachen, E. (2000) Merged and Unmerged Services: libraries and computing in the University of Wisconsin system. In Hardesty L.. (ed.), *Books, Bytes and Bridges: libraries and computer centers in academic institutions*, Chicago, American Library Association.

Molholt, P. (1989) What Happened to the Merger Debate? *Libraries and Computer Centers: Issues of Mutual Concern*, (May), 1–2.

Neff, R. (1985) Merging Libraries and Computer Centers: manifest destiny or manifestly deranged? *Educom Bulletin*, (winter), 8–16.

Neff, R. (2000) Merging the Library and the Computer Center: indications and contraindications. In Hardesty L. (ed.), *Books, Bytes and Bridges: libraries and computer centers in academic institutions*, Chicago, American Library Association.

Oke, L. (2003) *Planning for Information Technology in the Small College*, Bloomington, Indiana, Indiana University (Ed.D. dissertation).

Plane, R. (1981) Merging a Library and a Computer Center, *Perspectives in Computing*, (October), 14–21.

Rogers, E. M. (1995) Diffusion of Innovations, 4th edn, New York, The Free Press.

Seiden, P. and Kathman M. (2000) A History of the Rhetoric and Reality of Library and Computing Relationships. In Hardesty L. (ed.), *Books, Bytes and Bridges: libraries and computer centers in academic institutions*, Chicago, American Library Association.

Wagner, R. (2000) The Gettysburg Experience. In Hardesty L. (ed.), *Books, Bytes and Bridges: libraries and computer centers in academic institutions*, Chicago, American Library Association.

Young, A. (1994) Information Technology and Libraries: a virtual convergence, *Cause/Effect*, (fall), 5–6, 12.

Index

Please note that there are no index entries for either library or computing services in general. The inclusion of these in converged services is assumed and references to them appear extensively throughout the text. Please see Contents Page for universities appearing in case studies throughout this book.